SHAKESPEAREAN TRAGEDY

The problems posed by Shakespeare's great tragedies have challenged generations of critics and provoked a wide-ranging and varied critical reaction. In this book, Professor Dennis Bratchell provides a clear introductory guide through the maze of interpretation. He explains the development of Shakespeare criticism, selecting examples of original writing to illustrate the main lines of approach to Shakespearean tragedy. He shows how critical perceptions have changed from Renaissance to modern times, and helps the reader to develop an informed, individual response to Shakespeare's great tragedies.

An introductory chapter traces the development of tragedy from classical times to the time of Shakespeare. Carefully chosen extracts chart the changing emphasis from the neo-classical and Romantic, to approaches through character, performance studies, and language; a linking commentary maintains the continuity of the central theme. Each of the great tragedies is considered in turn, and a final chapter summarizes contemporary approaches so that the student can link the critical past with the present critical scene.

D. F. Bratchell was until recently Professor and Head of the Department of English at the University of Wales Institute of Science and Technology. He is now Professor Emeritus, University of Wales.

CRITICAL APPROACH SERIES

General editor: Donald Thomas

THE POST-ROMANTICS Donald Thomas
SHAKESPEAREAN TRAGEDY D.F. Bratchell

SHAKESPEAREAN TRAGEDY

◆

edited by D. F. BRATCHELL

LONDON AND NEW YORK

First published 1990 by Routledge
11 New Fetter Lane, London EC4P 4EE
29 West 35th Street, New York, NY 10001

Printed in Great Britain by
Richard Clay Ltd, Bungay, Suffolk

British Library Cataloguing in Publication Data
Bratchell, D. F. (Dennis Frank)
Shakespearean tragedy (Critical approach)
1. Drama in English. Shakespeare.
William, 1564–1616 *Tragedies*
I. Title   822.3'3

ISBN 0 415 03402 7 (hbk)
0 415 03403 5 (pbk)

Library of Congress Cataloging in Publication Data
Bratchell, D. F.
Shakespearean tragedy / D. F. Bratchell.
p.   cm. (–) (Critical approach)
Bibliography: p.
Includes index.
1. Shakespeare, William, 1564–1616. Tragedies.
I. Title.   II. Series.
PR2983.B728   1990
822.3'3(–)dc20   89–10506

And Man in portions can foresee
His own funereal destiny;
His wretchedness, and his resistance,
And his sad unallied existence:
To which his Spirit may oppose
Itself - and equal to all woes,
    And a firm will, and a deep sense,
Which even in torture can descry
    Its own concentered recompense,
Triumphant where it dares defy,
And making Death a Victory.

GEORGE GORDON NOEL, LORD BYRON,
Prometheus, Diodati, July 1816

Contents

Acknowledgements

We are grateful for permission given to reproduce extracts from the following:

G. Wilson Knight, *The Wheel of Fire*, Oxford University Press, 1930; Methuen: London, 1949, 1960.

Clifford Leech, *Shakespeare's Tragedies*, Chatto & Windus: London, 1950; reprinted 1975 Greenwood Press, Westport, Connecticut.

Caroline Spurgeon, *Shakespeare's Imagery and What it Tells Us*, Cambridge University Press, 1935, 1971.

J. I. M. Stewart, *Character and Motive in Shakespeare*, Longmans, Green & Co., 1949.

E. E. Stoll, *Art and Artifice in Shakespeare*, Cambridge University Press and Barnes & Noble: New York, 1933; Methuen, 1963.

J. Dover Wilson, *What Happens in Hamlet*, Cambridge University Press, 1935.

1

The development of tragedy

CLASSICAL TRAGEDY

Classical literary theory established tragedy and epic as the dominant literary forms, for which certain standards were defined and prescribed as necessary. Modern criticism is less certain about genres, at best seeing them as descriptive rather than prescriptive. Tragedy has passed through many interpretations in its long history, but has dominated recognized periods of literary excellence. Nowadays there are those who think tragedy is dead, while others discern its modern version in the works of writers like Henrik Ibsen and Arthur Miller. In the concept itself there is no lack of interest.

The legacy of the prescriptive nature of classical theory led to controversy when criticism attempted to impose classically inspired principles on literary practice. The situation was complicated by the emergence of new literary forms like prose fiction. In drama the difficulty of equating precept with practice led to the pedantic search for genre subdivisions. Polonius's famous outburst made the point: 'tragedy, comedy, history, pastoral, pastoral-comical, historical-pastoral, tragical-historical, tragical-comical-historical-pastoral, scene individable, or poem un-limited' (*Hamlet*, II, ii. 392–6). Shakespeare's implied comment on categorizing pedantry no doubt found a ready response from his audience. But however difficult tragedy is to define, Shakespeare's relationship to the genre is worth pursuing, not because he should have conformed to the theory but in order to illuminate his practice.

The student-notes which became the *Poetics* of Aristotle in *c.*330 BC provide an essential starting-point. This first work of literary criticism was essentially practical in its basic aims. Greek attitudes were all-embracing, and the *Poetics* has a moral as well as a literary aim. We may now be suspicious of literature which has designs upon

1

us, but we can recognize this aspect of Aristotle without dismissing him completely. He was known but largely misunderstood by the Middle Ages, and the Renaissance stressed dogma rather than literary insight. For Aristotle literature is knowledge, and his approach is systematic; he defines his terms, and analyses the constituent parts of his subject with scientific precision.

Aristotle's famous definition of tragedy describes it as the imitation of an action which is serious, complete, and has magnitude; an action, that is, which is not merely trivial. The medium of tragedy is a language which is embellished with artistic ornamentation, such as melody or poetic diction. The mode employed by tragedy is dramatic, not narrative, the story unfolded by persons acting as characters who excite pity and fear, providing (for the auditors) an outlet for these emotions which effects a purgation and a sense of pleasurable relief. Aristotle's notion of 'catharsis', or a clearance of the emotions which is pleasurable and beneficial, needs to be viewed against the background of Plato's strictures on art in general and poetry in particular. One of Plato's views on art was that it could produce a dangerous incontinence of emotions leading to violent outbursts which were damaging to public morality.

In his analysis of the constituent parts of tragedy Aristotle lists, in order of importance, plot, character, thought, diction, song or melody, and spectacle. The primary importance of plot is insisted upon, and this is described as the life and soul of tragedy, taking precedence over character, which became so much the concern of later criticism, particularly of Shakespearean tragedy. The analysis of plot is detailed and thorough, and it is clear that Aristotle's view of plot, defined as the imitation of an important action, is above all the requirement for evidence of an overall design or structural unity, without distraction or unnecessary digression. The organic nature of the whole, it is argued, should be such that no element can be removed without destroying the unity. This unity of action was later to be a matter for critical argument, for example over the comedy element in *Hamlet*, but it is clear that by plot Aristotle meant far more than the mere skeleton of a story, and modern critics who dismiss this stress on plot in the drama have not always grasped the details of the case. Ideally the plot should concentrate on one issue, centred on the character of the tragic hero, but necessarily involving other characters. Aristotle lists the plot situations which should be avoided: the good man passing from happiness to misery, because that is neither fear-inspiring nor piteous, and is merely odious; the bad man passing from misery to happiness, because this does not appeal to our emotions of pity and fear, our sense of poetic justice; an extremely bad man falling from happiness to misery, because pity is only aroused by an undeserved misfortune and fear by the predicament of one who is like ourselves. Hence the tragic hero for Aristotle is an intermediate person, not pre-eminently virtuous and just, whose misfortune is brought about not by his vice or depravity but by some error of judgment.

Aristotle's view of character was essentially to see it as part of the plot. As we shall see, this contrasts with a later view of Shakespearean character in tragedy, where characters were extrapolated from drama and given a life of their own. A difficult point to appreciate is Aristotle's insistence on the portrayal of good characters. Greek drama was on the grand scale, with strong religious overtones, and even minor characters had to be on the heroic scale with the good elements in each character being brought out. Changes in stage conditions and the circumstances of the drama allowed more freedom in later times, but Aristotle's view of character still serves as a reminder that unredeemed villains and spotless heroines belong to melodrama not tragedy. Characters should be appropriate to the plot, realistic and believable, and develop consistently. Unlike later critics of Shakespearean tragedy, Aristotle does not see the elements in isolation: the words and actions of each person represented in the play should be the logical outcome of the character, just as the incidents of the play are the logical outcome of the whole situation. Aristotelian tragedy may be larger than life, but it is not founded on improbabilities, and as with skilful portraiture character delineation may accentuate certain features in the service of a central plot or theme without losing likeness or credibility.

Most of the other elements in tragedy specified by Aristotle are concerned with Greek rhetoric, except spectacle. He places spectacle last, admitting that it can arouse the emotions of pity and fear, but insisting that the true pleasure of tragedy does not require its aid. In his council of moderation Aristotle warns against allowing either spectacle or character undue emphasis.

RENAISSANCE CRITICAL THEORIES

Despite changes in literary form and social context, Aristotle's criticism remains a valuable guide, if the pedantic accretions can be brushed off. The pedantries began early in the Renaissance when critical theorists seized upon Aristotle's text as the basis of literary prescription for a new age. They formulated a set of rules, particularly the so-called rules of the unities of time, place, and action. From the Renaissance onwards arguments about the unities have been a persistent theme in approaches to tragedy, including Shakespearean tragedy. The rules have little basis in Aristotle's formulation for tragedy, but the neo-classical argument does not resolve itself into a simple division between disciplined classicism on the one hand and Romantic freedom on the other. There is no simple polarization between Racine and Shakespeare.

Aristotle's one unity is carefully explained and justified in the *Poetics*, and that is the unity of action. By the sixteenth century Italian writers like Castalvetro were insisting that this meant the action must occupy a space of time no more than twelve hours long, and must be confined to one location. French critics like Boileau and Le Bossu, codifying rules of reason in the intellectual climate of the seventeenth century and labelling them Aristotelian, argued for adherence to the rules of place, time, and action to ensure verisimilitude. French attitudes become understandable if we examine the historical development of European drama, but it was unfortunate that instances like Voltaire's castigation of Shakespeare for his lack of knowledge of the rules and uncouth barbarity should have helped to polarize attitudes on nationalistic grounds.

ELIZABETHAN TRAGEDIES

Ben Jonson epitomizes the English writer of the Shakespearean period who upheld the virtues of classical decorum. His qualified praise of Shakespeare with his (by comparison) 'small Latin and less Greek' is well known, but for all Jonson's learned insistence on classical authority his common-sense attitude to precepts is a warning against neo-classical pedantry: 'No precepts', he writes, in *Timber, or Discoveries*, 'will profit a fool.' Sir Philip Sidney's *Apology for Poetry* was a defence of literature against the Puritans, but his use of what he understood of classical literary theory indicates the nature of classical influence in the sixteenth century in England. When he considers English drama he acknowledges that *Gorboduc* heightened Senecan style and morality, but as a model is deficient because it lacks the unities of time and place. Writers of English tragedy certainly owed more to the Roman writer Seneca than to the precepts of Aristotle.

The nine tragedies attributed to Seneca derived from Greek originals but without the religious background, and although probably not written for performance offered distinctively theatrical elements of stories of revenge, ghosts, and grand guignol horrors. The neo-classical tradition persisted in the Inns of Court and the universities, and even in the early seventeenth century Ben Jonson, with his plays *Sejanus* and *Catiline*, hoped to rival his great contemporary Shakespeare. Writers for the public theatre selected more freely from classical sources, largely ignoring precepts but borrowing Senecan structure with modifications like the use of Dumb Show rather than Chorus, and from *Gorboduc* onwards using English blank verse as the poetic medium.

The development of tragedy in English drama in the sixteenth century is not simply a rejection of neo-classical theory, and an uninhibited display of Romantic freedom. Elizabethan playwrights adapted and developed for their own purposes classical form and structure, but it was the classical impetus which led to their bringing a heightened style to the public theatres. Although the humanists struggled for a neo-classical decorum, the more successful plays in the public theatre blended Romantic freedom with classical restraint. In particular, the revenge theme, with its origins in the classics, was exploited with remarkable and well-attested success in Kyd's *Spanish Tragedy*. In this play, Senecan form is brought alive theatrically, so that the stage conventions of revenge, passionate intrigue, madness, and the supernatural, with some subtlety of character delineation, provide a dramatic external action to capture an audience. Significant dramatic possibilities, not least the theme of the hesitant revenger, were all later to be developed in Shakespearean tragedy. Departure from Greek mythology as source material for tragedy is encouraged by the popular dramatization of history in the chronicle history-plays. These plays bear the marks of Senecan form and the morality tradition, but their popularity on the public stage reflects the Elizabethan liking for Romantic incident and exciting external action. Shakespeare's handling of historical themes, in plays with precipitate stage-action, his new insights in the character development of the main protagonists, and expressive use of poetic dialogue provided him with important elements of his approach to tragedy.

Of the many playwrights in the late sixteenth century Christopher Marlowe, who, in Ben Jonson's phrase, developed the 'mighty line' of English dramatic blank verse, above all points the way toward a distinctive Shakespearean tragedy. Marlowe's lyrically charged and passionate verse depicts strongly developed heroic central figures who express individual worth and vaulting ambition rather than princely misfortune. For Marlowe, the appeal of the tragic hero is in the nobility of the struggle, not in the moral lesson of the downfall from prosperity. With *Doctor Faustus* he also portrays with lyrical intensity the psychology of the inner struggle, and in his *Edward II* suggests the tragic pathos of an historical figure subjected to powerful rival forces in the turbulent action of chronicle history. Marlowe's brilliant use of blank verse needed to be adapted to a more varied dramatic structure, and his exploitation of dramatic incident more firmly controlled, but his contribution to the development of an English approach to tragedy is undeniable. Commentators have frequently isolated Shakespeare from his age, and treated him as a natural genius ignorant of the rules or as an alienated Romantic with a vision beyond his time. This is completely to misunderstand the nature of his stature as a dramatist, and the creative milieu which characterized his age. As a dramatist he needed the opportunity to communicate with a responsive audience, and as a writer he needed the stimulating environment of literary creativity. In the public theatres Shakespeare had at hand the raw material for an approach to tragedy uninhibited by classical rules but retaining the essence of the golden age.

Shakespeare's achievement in tragedy was not the work of an eccentric genius whose natural talent flourished in an undisciplined age, and critical approaches to his work in the genre have often been mistaken in not realizing that he was of his age as well as for all time. From his contemporaries and the opportunities provided in the theatre of his own time, he was able to weave the various strands of the drama into his own rich and varied approach to tragedy. The compelling inevitability of a revenge theme with its dramatic suspense – the theatrical excitement of external action – and, matching this, the subtle insights into character interplay and the exploitation of English blank verse and dramatic prose are all facets of Shakespeare's mastery of his craft. Experimentation with existing forms and the development of new forms of dramatic structure are characteristic of Shakespeare's plays from the outset of his career. In tragedy the early *Titus Andronicus* exploits stage horrors and Senecan revenge, but gives way to lyrical intensity and a Renaissance *tour de force* with the star-crossed lovers of *Romeo and Juliet*. The fateful passion of love tragedy is brought to new heights in the historical theme of *Antony and Cleopatra*, and in his English history plays and Roman plays he explores the tragic potential of a central character. The four great tragedies of *Hamlet*, *Othello*, *King Lear*, and *Macbeth*, which belong to the period of Shakespeare's growing mastery at the turn of the century, do not constitute an exploitation of a successful formula he has at last reached. Each is distinctive in penetrating further depths in tragedy, and their individual nature has often taxed critics who have attempted to encapsulate Shakespearean tragedy in an all-embracing orthodoxy. *Hamlet* exploits the dramatic possibilities of the revenge theme which was already popular but gives it greater purpose, and develops the stock trait of melancholia in the central character in a way which has fascinated commentators ever since. From the treatment of revenge with its fated prince Shakespeare turns to the domestic tragedy of a non-royal, non-white person in *Othello*, using a tight-knit dramatic structure which is almost neo-classical. Domestic tragedies had been popularized by other writers, but Shakespeare gives the emotional turmoil of jealousy, the agonizing interplay of ambition and envy, a truly tragic dimension of universal significance. In contrast to the controlled dramatic form of *Othello*, the loose and episodic structure of the old chronicle history form in *King Lear* has been viewed by critics as a retrogression in dramatic terms, as perverse and unactable as its central character. Yet other critics have hailed this as Shakespeare's supreme masterpiece, a dramatic poem unsurpassed in its relentless probing of new reaches in tragedy, with truly epic qualities and imaginative grandeur. The central figure of the singular hero is replaced in *Macbeth* by the compelling relationship between an ambitious general and his scheming wife in an unholy partnership of murder. As the tragic hero becomes a figure of evil, a Marlovian awareness of the consequences of the central act intensifies the dramatic tension. The dark atmosphere of despair, the exploitation of the supernatural, the overt political theme and plot, give yet a different emphasis to tragedy. Shakespeare's achievement in tragedy was not the fulfilment of a preconceived design or the response to classical precepts, but a creative exploitation of the opportunities provided by the genre.

NEO-CLASSICAL CRITICISM

Critical approaches to Shakespearean tragedy in the seventeenth and early eighteenth centuries were dominated by the theories of neo-classicism. Critics either went to considerable lengths to demonstrate how Shakespeare violated Aristotelian rules, or recognized the force of his accomplishment and sought ways of explaining his success in spite of his lack of conformity with a classical system. The very excesses of the attack by a critic like Thomas Rymer, who castigated Shakespeare in his *Short View of Tragedy*, indicate the intransigence of the problem of fitting Shakespearean tragedy into a conforming pattern. The familiar Aristotelian precepts are cited: Shakespeare violates the unities, his characters do not sufficiently stress the good and morally uplifting, the death of a Desdemona offends poetic justice, Shakespeare's language moves from the extremes of high rhetoric to mere quibbling, and he juxtaposes lofty tragedy and lowly comedy. There is a positive side to these attacks: the classical argument encourages close consideration of the texts, critical discussion is rationally sustained, not merely the selection of passages for sentimental praise. That the neo-classical background could foster a more balanced approach is illustrated by the criticism of a far greater critic than Rymer, the dramatist and poet John Dryden.

As a writer Dryden himself came under the influence of the classically aligned French mood of the English restoration period; he wrote plays in the popular form of heroic tragedies in rhyming couplets for much of his career. As a critic he balances theory with creativity, and he has no time for pedantry, disagreeing, in his 'An Essay of Dramatic Poesy', with the rigidity of the French with their 'servile observation of the unities'. In his own work he eventually abandoned the rhyming couplet, so long regarded as the English equivalent of the French alexandrine, and turned to Shakespeare's medium of English blank verse for his greatest tragedy, *All for Love*. In his preface he pays genuine homage to Shakespeare, admits his prejudice that the Elizabethan age was less refined than his own, and makes his own distinctive approach to the tragedy.

Dryden, who died in 1700, was writing from the standpoint of a period which was reacting against the supposed barbarity of the former age. His comments are a valuable touchstone, justifying Dr Johnson's claim that he was the father of English criticism. He drew heavily on French critical theory, but he develops a sustained critical argument which is essentially open-minded and positive. Dryden's recognition of Shakespeare's genius is genuine, although he found it difficult at times to effect a satisfactory compromise between classical theory and Shakespearean practice, particularly in tragedy. Apart from his positive handling of neo-classical theory, Dryden also brings the first-hand knowledge of the theatrical practitioner to his Shakespearean criticism.

THE AGE OF JOHNSON

In the eighteenth century critical approaches to Shakespearean tragedy became essentially literary. It became the practice also to adapt Shakespeare's plays to bring them into line with classical decorum and what was assumed to be theatrical taste. The great actor-manager David Garrick adapted Shakespeare to both fashionable and popular taste, and his individual control of production and performance established a theatrical practice which continued into the nineteenth century. The literary treatment of Shakespearean tragedy was modelled on the criticism of classical texts, and the establishment and exegesis of texts became an important part of Shakespearean scholarship with the work of Nicholas Rowe and the numerous editors of Shakespeare from Pope and Theobald to Dr Johnson. Later in the eighteenth century the work of Edward Capell and George Steevens brought new levels of scholarship to the study of Shakespeare, and textual work on the plays ranged through both Folio and Quarto editions. Inevitably criticism became allied to scholarship, and the elevation of Shakespeare's texts to classical status meant that tragedy was approached from the study rather than the theatre.

The arguments over Shakespeare and the rules of the unities continued with the refutation of Thomas Rymer's extreme attitudes by critics like Charles Gildon. There were many who accepted the undoubted power of Shakespeare's approach to tragedy, but hesitated between acclaiming him as an individual genius or arguing for his place within the classical orthodoxy which dominated the eighteenth century. There was no lack of praise of Shakespearean tragedy, with a significant and prophetic emphasis on Shakespeare's ability to create characters who revealed the warmth and depth of human understanding. A French attack on Shakespeare's unnatural and extravagant handling of tragedy was answered by William Guthrie, who introduced a note of comparative criticism by contrasting the living appeal of Shakespeare's tragic creations with the lifeless artificiality of English neo-classical portrayals. The most authoritative statement of eighteenth-century attitudes to neo-classicism is by the giant of the period, Dr Samuel Johnson. The Preface to *The Plays of William Shakespeare* is a landmark in criticism, although Johnson's edition of Shakespeare was a long time in preparation and has disappointed Shakespearean scholars. Johnson's statement of the neo-classical position allows him to bring his high style and critical authority to raise the level of the debate, and his moderate summing-up of the argument over the unities is obviously important in relation to Shakespearean tragedy. There are times when Johnson himself in his fulsome recognition of Shakespeare's individual genius is in danger of encouraging the strain of exaggerated praise already emerging and which was to be labelled 'bardolatry'. But in tragedy Johnson found Shakespeare wanting, for his mingling of comedy and tragedy and for his failure always to sustain a moral standpoint. The prejudices of his critical terms of reference are clear in Johnson, but there is often warmth and sensitivity in his response to Shakespeare, and his stimulating impact as a major critic illustrates the problem confronting neo-classicism faced with the creative energy of Shakespearean tragedy.

By the end of the eighteenth century Shakespeare had been raised to classic status *par excellence*. The language of bardolatry now truly emerges, and he is described as an astonishing phenomenon of world status with superlatives lavished freely. The hyperbole extended to Shakespearean tragedy, notwithstanding Dr Johnson, and Shakespeare was held to have surpassed the Greeks at their greatest. Even at the time, there were those who cautioned against this surfeit of praise, and realized that substituting emotion for reason did little service to Shakespeare. In a sense this was perhaps a reaction against the aridities of the critical arguments of neo-classicism. Nevertheless, despite Dr Johnson's authoritative condemnation of pedantic excess in his view of the unities, the neo-classical debate continued in critical approaches. The intense interest in Shakespeare and the search for new ways of interpretation led to the use of biography, encouraged by scholars like Edmund Malone who mingled historical fact and inference from the works to present a sentimentalized picture of Shakespeare the man. This subjective mingling of fact and fiction, illustrating the persistent lure of the cult of personality, continues in some criticism.

CHARACTER ANALYSIS

The difficulty of reconciling Shakespeare's achievement in tragedy with the supposed rules of classical orthodoxy explains the desire for interpretations with a different emphasis. Arguments continued over instances such as the blinding of Gloucester in *King Lear* as a gratuitous spectacle of horror, the non-Aristotelian criminality of the hero in *Macbeth*, the irregularities of plot in *Hamlet*, and the apparently excessive malevolence of Iago, coupled with Desdemona's unnecessary onstage murder, in *Othello*. Shakespeare's bawdiness and his questionable morality are cited against him well before nineteenth-century attempts to clean up the text. Traditional approaches by no means led to agreed conclusions, and the same plays or situations were seen as moral by some and immoral by others; critical approaches often reveal more about the critics than about the works under scrutiny. The critical atmosphere of the late eighteenth century was not simply divided between those for and those against the classical approach to Shakespearean tragedy. There were neo-classicists who praised Shakespeare's ability to adapt the rules to his native genius, and others who argued pragmatically that he was the exception who had no need for rules. The widespread recognition of the compelling power of Shakespearean tragedy led to an understandable search for new emphases in critical appraisal. Many strands of criticism continued into the nineteenth century, but the explanation of Shakespeare's distinctive creative power was seen more and more in his ability to depict human character.

An early example of this emphasis on Shakespeare's handling of character is provided by Thomas Whately, who in 'Remarks on Some of the Characters of Shakespeare' argues for a change of emphasis toward the study of character – 'a subject for criticism more worthy of attention than the common topics of discussion'. Whately, in this fragment of a book on Shakespeare's characters he had planned to write, compares the handling of the characters of Richard III and Macbeth, and notes particularly the deep insight and distinguishing power of Shakespeare's portrayal compared with the lifeless generalities of English attempts at classical form. It is easy to see how the approach to character in neo-classical tragedy derives from Aristotle's precepts for a larger-than-life figure harnessed to the tragic theme, but Whately's analysis recognizes Shakespeare's handling of character as breathing new life into an old form. Unfortunately, these beginnings of character emphasis were to be exaggerated into a preoccupation with character abstracted from other elements, which ignored not only the precepts of Aristotle but the nature of drama itself. An influential essay encouraging this tendency, hailed as a landmark in character analysis, was Maurice Morgann's detailed defence of Falstaff from the charge of cowardice, published as 'An Essay on the Dramatic Character of Sir John Falstaff'. Morgann's essay is part of the critical debate which applied psychological realism to the analysis of favourite characters such as Hamlet and Falstaff, but his general remarks on Shakespeare's characters and what can be inferred about them encouraged the tendency to view dramatic character as independent reality. There were certainly those who denied the possibility of fictionalizing completely the subtleties of human behaviour, but the critical fashion developed of attacking or defending characters, particularly in terms of their consistency of behaviour and moral purpose. Shakespearean tragedy is rich in characters whose moral interpretation provides subject for argument, and the nineteenth-century concern with moral standards coupled with the rise of the realistic novel encouraged a critical approach through character. Although some critics continued to examine the interplay between plot and character, the psychological realism of tragic character apprehended from the text was easier to relate to prose fiction than to Aristotelian drama.

THE ROMANTICS AND TRAGEDY

The Romantic period did not bring about a sudden change in the critical appraisal of Shakespearean tragedy, but the literary enthusiasts for the new climate of freedom from classically dominated restraint found in Shakespeare a new hero and a change in critical approach was encouraged. In the late eighteenth century the German reaction against rationalism had manifested itself in the literary movement known as *Sturm und Drang* (or 'Storm and Stress', taken from the title of a contemporary novel), and for many Germans Shakespeare epitomized the natural genius who carried the true spirit of tragedy, rather than the French disciples of Aristotle hitherto held as exemplary. Critics like G. E. Lessing, and the great German poet Goethe, acknowledged the overwhelming effect upon them of the beauty and power of Shakespeare's writing. Significantly, Lessing argued for a new interpretation of the *Poetics*, and urged the study of the plays of both the Greeks and Shakespeare rather than the cold preoccupation with the abstractions of theory. Shakespeare's works were translated into German, notably by A. W. Schlegel, and Shakespearean tragedy was admired not only for its dramatic impact but for its philosophical depth and its suggestion of mysterious power. Shakespeare provided an ideal focus for Romantic fervour, and his tragedies were hailed as both intellectually stimulating and emotionally disturbing. Schlegel writes, in *On Dramatic Art and Literature*, of his admiration for Shakespeare's power of character delineation and ability to evoke the mysterious world of the spirit: 'this Prometheus not merely forms men, he opens up the gate of the magic world of spirits; calls up the midnight ghost; exhibits before us his witches amidst their unhallowed mysteries; peoples the air with sportive fairies and sylphs.' We have here a revelation of the taste which would respond to the Romantic world of Wagner. In a significant passage, in view of later directions in criticism, Lessing praises Shakespeare's ability to portray not only the secrets and passions of love, but also the dark manifestations of mental disorder. Lessing's comment on Shakespeare's depiction of melancholy in a character like Hamlet – as being so accurate that doctors could learn from him – indicates an ominous trend in the criticism of tragedy. In an extraordinary display of Romantic fervour Shakespeare was adopted by the German literary world, which even claimed that it comprehended him better than did those in his native country and language.

English critics like Hazlitt and Coleridge were not always keen to acknowledge the German Romantic influence, but they adopted the spirit of the new German approach in their criticism. Charles Lamb's plea for a liberal imaginative approach to Shakespearean tragedy took a distinctive line by arguing for the freedom to interpret the plays unfettered by the intervention of stage production. This view may seem extreme to modern commentators, but it must be seen in the context of early nineteenth-century stage-productions which were artificially adapted to the proscenium-arch theatre with its elaborate scenery and very little understanding of the constraints of the Elizabethan theatre. Lamb's arguments for making Shakespeare a special case are interesting, and have been too readily dismissed in our own time, when theatre productions still require critical appraisal.

Samuel Taylor Coleridge is one of the greatest of Shakespearean critics, still worth consulting in the twentieth century. He established a critical synthesis which took the new currents of the Romantic period and developed an approach which was neither traditionally hidebound nor enthusiastically undiscriminating. From the outset Coleridge demonstrated that Shakespeare's handling of tragedy was not a haphazard and ignorant freedom from any rules, but a judiciously controlled development of form organically conceived and suited to its purpose. As a poet Coleridge responded to Shakespeare's poetic genius applied creatively in the plays as well as the poems. Like the Germans, and reflecting a classical theme, Coleridge coupled Shakespeare's poetic power with his philosophical power. In this sense Coleridge argues for the recognition of Shakespearean tragedy as having some of the essential attributes of classical Greek tragedy, concerned with the ultimate questions about human destiny. At times Coleridge's liking for philosophical digressions, his tendency to probe the metaphysical, taxes the reader. It is, however, perhaps because he was himself a creative writer that he saw that Shakespeare's accomplishment was not merely naturally inspired and Romantically unique, but a sustained process of artistic development.

Thomas De Quincey's famous essay 'On the Knocking at the Gate in Macbeth' exemplifies the critical tendency to examine specific situations. He imaginatively pursues the tragic repercussions of the central act of darkness, and demonstrates the importance of dramatic context in the approach to Shakespearean tragedy. William Hazlitt brings Romantic enthusiasm to the criticism of tragedy, but strikes an important chord in stressing the emotional appeal of the poetry in Shakespeare's plays. He goes beyond mere character evaluation, and adopts an interpretative and illustrated approach to the poetry of the text which is forward looking in its method. Hazlitt is no mere idolizer, and gives the familiar list of supposed faults, but catches the essence of Shakespearean tragedy by recognizing its universal appeal to audiences.

THE VICTORIANS

Criticism was not notably developed by the Victorians but there was considerable increase in Shakespearean scholarship in the period, and Shakespeare's plays and the context of his life and times were closely scrutinized. The chronology of the plays was reasonably established, and the influence of the Romantic movement, with its stress on the philosophical unity of creativity and interpretation, was continued with attempts to establish the successive 'periods' of Shakspeare's development as an artist. Edward Dowden's *Shakspere: A Critical Study of his Mind and Art* endeavours to identify the periods of Shakespeare's personal development with the periods of his creativity beginning in 1590, 1600, and 1610 respectively. According to this Romantic view, by 1600 Shakespeare, like Hamlet, had been tested by personal experience, and had reached the philosophical insight and artistic maturity which would enable him to write *Othello*, *King Lear*, and *Macbeth*. *Hamlet* constituted the great turning-point: 'the point of departure in Shakspere's immense and final sweep of mind, that in which he endeavoured to include and comprehend life for the first time adequately' (p. 222). The philosophical strand in Dowden's criticism was to be continued, and seriously applied to character study, but the sentimental aspects of his idealized picture of Shakespeare the man was to encourage a biographical interpretation of the tragedies and sonnets still persistent. Theatrical production began to pay more attention to the historical circumstances of the Elizabethan theatre, but the rise of the actor-manager encouraged concentration on the starring roles of popular characters, and by modern standards productions were stylized and encumbered with scenery. In some hands character study became absurdly exaggerated, and whereas De Quincey had demonstrated the skilful handling of female character in the tragedies, works like Mrs Cowden Clarke's *Girlhood of Shakespeare's Heroines* represented a sentimental view of character far removed from its dramatic context. In contrast, A. C. Bradley's *Shakespearean Tragedy* was neither sentimental nor Romantic, and is characterized by its philosophical standpoint and the detailed analysis of the psychology of the major characters. It is unfortunate that the critical reaction from Bradley in the twentieth century – largely because he appeared to give academic respectability to psychological naturalism and the non-theatrical cult of character – led for some time to the neglect of his contribution to the study of Shakespearean tragedy. His work is the most important critical legacy from the end of the Victorian period.

FREUD AND THE THEATRE

Studies in Elizabethan theatre were intensified after the discovery of the drawing of the Swan theatre in 1888, and this, coupled with the increasing use of bibliographical techniques in the establishment of Shakespeare's text, led in the twentieth century to a new emphasis on the historical context of Shakespeare's plays. The possibility of a return to the theatrical presentation of Shakespearean tragedy, without the inappropriate interruption of act- and scene-divisions and with a corresponding exploitation of a platform (non-proscenium) stage, meant that literary critics were more inclined than hitherto to criticize Shakespeare as a dramatist. Early in the century scholars like Sir Walter Raleigh in his study *Shakespeare*, although not entirely free from the intentional fallacy and assertions about Shakespeare's motivation in tragedy, try to make a more objective approach than the Victorians with their autobiographical speculations. It is ironic that although there was a reaction from the emphasis on character, the impetus given to the study of the psychology of human behaviour by the work of Sigmund Freud should lead to the ultimate non-theatrical treatment of tragic character in Dr Ernest Jones's 'Oedipus Complex as an Explanation of Hamlet's Mystery'. Although the general trend in Shakespeare studies was against the artificial extrapolation of character, the post-Freudian preoccupation with psychological naturalism is a recurring element in criticism. Writers as well as literary critics exploit their apprehension of Freudian psychology, but it is remarkable how Shakespeare's tragic characters have satisfied the layman's pre-Freudian observations of human behaviour as well as the scientific objectivity of post-Freudian analyses.

There is an interesting parallel to the development of the psychological approach in dramatic criticism in the emergence of the acting method originating with the Russian Theatre Director Constantin Stanislavski of the Moscow Arts Theatre. Stanislavski stressed group-playing as against the star system, and sought to establish a more subtle method of performance by developing the inner awareness of the actor in tune with the psychological motivation of dramatic character. Unfortunately this approach was somewhat discredited by the exaggerated version known as The Method which almost made a virtue of inarticulacy, but in general more subtle and imaginative approaches to acting and production have been introduced in the twentieth century. The theatrical interpretation of Shakespearean tragedy has revealed new richness in the texts, and has introduced into criticism Stanislavski's concept of subtext, the deeper meanings which flow continuously beneath the surface words of the play. Change from the declamatory style of acting and appropriate methods of staging have encouraged the interpretation of tragic character in true dramatic context. Shakespeare's ability to reveal conscious and subconscious reaction beneath the spoken word is explored in complementary critical and theatrical approaches.

THE 'REALISTS'

With the interest in Shakespeare's theatre came a fresh examination of his audience, and more emphasis on the historical approach. It had long been a view of Shakespeare's handling of tragedy that he was the victim of circumstances, that his approach could be explained by the fact that he had to write down to the level of an uncultivated audience. The German scholar Levin Ludwig Schücking, one of whose works appeared in English as *Character Problems in Shakespeare's Plays*, argued that a realistic assessment of Shakespeare's achievement showed that he was using old, established stage-techniques, such as the soliloquy and a loose episodic structure, because he was merely responding to popular taste and exploiting established theatrical practice. This emphasis on Shakespeare as a master of stagecraft, and essentially a popular entertainer, was a denial of the need for the psychological subtleties and philosophical pretensions of Bradley's view of the tragedies.

Muriel Bradbrook developed this approach in *Themes and Conventions of Elizabethan Tragedy*: the Elizabethans did not construct alternatives to classical rules, but used stock dramatic devices, which in the hands of the greatest writers became conventions; the essential structure of the plays is in words, not character or narrative, since the greatest dramatists were poets. Even Shakespeare's characters were subject to conventions of type and situation, defined by decorum and the theory of humours. Conventions included the credibility of slander, the impenetrability of disguise, and the limitations of motive. The Machiavellian Italian is commonplace in Elizabethan tragedy, as is the villain-hero typified by the conquering amoral hero of Marlowe's *Tamburlaine*. The relevance to Iago and Macbeth is clear.

The American scholar E. E. Stoll became the most influential figure in the 'realistic' school of criticism of Shakespeare through theatre history, and in *Art and Artifice in Shakespeare* he asserts that it was not the psychological realism of character that was so important in the plays but the psychological reaction of Shakespeare's audience. What in Shakespeare's text may seem absurd is easily accepted in the unfolding action of theatrical performance, and Shakespeare exploits his art and manipulates his audience reaction to create not life but an illusion.

POETRY AND LANGUAGE

The realist approach produced some reaction in further support of Bradley, but it also stimulated the search for new interpretations of the tragedies. G. Wilson Knight in *The Wheel of Fire* accepted that Shakespeare's plays were not a slice of life to be considered through psychological naturalism, but he looked for more than theatrical artifice. Concentrating on the individual texts, he argued for the discovery in each tragedy of a dominating theme, such as the conflict of life and death in *Macbeth*. This moved the emphasis from the theatre to poetry and language.

Much twentieth-century criticism has been concerned with the poetry of Shakespearean tragedy and close study of the texts, complemented by the burgeoning scholarship in textual studies. The language of Shakespeare's plays has been closely studied from various aspects, but the most fruitful linguistic approach to tragedy has been the work on imagery. Psychoanalysis and word-association techniques gave new impetus to a strand of criticism which had begun in the seventeenth century. Caroline Spurgeon's *Shakespeare's Imagery and What it Tells Us* used quantitative analysis to bring a quasi-scientific objectivity to the appraisal of the significance of imagery in the plays. The counting and classification of image-clusters led to the conclusion that particular plays have dominating images which establish a particular atmosphere or theme. The most famous example, in the realm of tragedy, is the symbolic iteration of images of disease in *Hamlet*. This conclusion has been criticized because it was extended to the supposed revelation of Shakespeare's own state of mind and treats language in isolation from its dramatic significance. The German writer Wolfgang Clemen adopted a more integrated approach to the study of imagery, but Caroline Spurgeon's pioneering work created an awareness of the linguistic aspects of Shakespearean tragedy and has had an enduring influence.

A corrective to the extreme swing against Bradley's approach to Shakespearean tragedy came with H. B. Charlton's *Shakespearian Tragedy* and J. I. M. Stewart's *Character and Motive in Shakespeare*. Both writers urge a new appraisal of the place of character study, rejecting the extremes of the realist school of criticism and urging a more sensitive reading of the poetry of Shakespeare's plays in the search for a new synthesis.

Clifford Leech returns to the relationship between classical and Shakespearean tragedy in *Shakespeare's Tragedies*, and he sees the catharsis of Aristotle in the balance of or opposition between terror and pride in Shakespeare. The tragic heroes in Shakespeare may conform with the Aristotelian mean, but the Greek sense of an all-powerful providence is lacking. In Shakespearean tragedy the hero is faced with the agonizing choice of individual responsibility, with no simple prescriptive message of assurance. This distinctive feature of personal decision, it is argued, is one reason for the intense interest in character in critical approaches to Shakespeare.

By the mid-twentieth century some of the critical approaches to Shakespearean tragedy from the seventeenth and eighteenth centuries still continued. Neo-classicism no longer dominated, but Shakespeare's relationship to the classical world remained of critical concern. The approach to character had changed its emphasis, stressing dramatic context but remaining central to many critical arguments. Psychology remained an enduring preoccupation, but considered for its relevance to the theatre rather than the clinic. More and more critical attention is directed at the theatrical effectiveness of Shakespearean tragedy, not only in historical terms but also in its manifestations in modern production.

The range of Shakespearean scholarship has become overwhelming, but although textual criticism and exegesis are specialist industries Shakespearean tragedy retains a universal appeal, extended by some successful attempts to convey it through the medium of cinema and television. It is much more difficult now than formerly to discern any critical consensus, but the plays themselves have displayed remarkable durability.

Shakespeare wrote a series of plays which have been categorized as tragedies, and four of those plays, which belong to his central period, are recognized as his great tragedies. For a particular audience, and in a particular theatre, Shakespeare applied his creative awareness to the tragic mode and his playwright's skill to different sets of source material. It is unlikely that he had any intention of establishing a stereotype or of exemplifying prescriptive standards; the evidence is that he was for ever exploring and experimenting with the essence of tragedy, unmindful of theory but excited by theatrical possibility.

The Greece of Aristotle had its own reasons for representing the universal good and the morally applicable *exemplum* in a very different sort of public theatre, and Shakespeare was a world away from classical Athens. Yet in his exploration of the ramifications of a significant plot or action, his creation of dramatic characters which provoked and continue to provoke human response, his stimulating mastery of language and stage situation, Shakespeare captures what is enduring about the spirit of Aristotle's *Poetics*. It is in this sense that we can recognize what is for convenience labelled 'Shakespearean tragedy', which has emerged remarkably unscathed through neoclassicism, bardolatry, character analysis, censure and censorship and the changing fashions across the years of critical approaches.

2

Critics and Shakespearean tragedy

Aristotle
Poetics (*c*.330 BC, printed 1536)

In his prescription for tragedy Aristotle lists its constituent parts, but clearly stresses the centrality of fable or plot. Nowhere does he define the rules of the unities, and character is not dismissed as of little importance but placed within the perspective of the overall action. This accords more with modern approaches to Shakespearean character than the exaggerations of psychological realism. Deep involvement in the emotions of pity and fear is more important for Aristotle than the superficial appeal of spectacle.

A tragedy, then, is the imitation of an action that is serious, has magnitude, and is complete in itself; in language with pleasurable accessories, each kind brought in separately in the various parts of the work; in a dramatic, not in a narrative form; with incidents arousing pity and fear, wherewith to accomplish its catharsis of such emotions . . .

There are six parts consequently of every tragedy, which determine its quality, viz. Plot, Character, Diction, Thought, Spectacle and Melody; two of them arising from the means, one from the manner, and three from the objects of the dramatic imitation; and there is nothing else besides these six. Of these elements, then, practically all of the dramatists have made use, as all plays alike admit of Spectacle, Character, Plot, Diction, Melody and Thought.

The most important of the six is the combination of the incidents of the story. Tragedy is essentially an imitation not of persons but of action and life, of happiness and misery. All human happiness or misery takes the form of action; the end aimed at is a certain kind of activity, not a quality. Character gives us qualities, but it is in our actions – what we do – that we are happy or the reverse. In a play accordingly they do not act in order to portray the characters; they include the characters for the sake of the action. So that it is the action in it, i.e. its Fable or Plot, that is the end and purpose of the tragedy; and the end is everywhere the chief thing. Besides this, a tragedy is impossible without action, but there may be one without character . . .

We maintain, therefore, that the first essential, the life and soul, so to speak, of tragedy, is the plot; and that the characters come second – compare the parallel in painting, where the most beautiful colours laid on without order will not give one the same pleasure as a simple black and white sketch of a portrait. We maintain that tragedy is primarily an imitation of action, and that it is mainly for the sake of the action that it imitates the personal agents. Third comes the element of thought, i.e. the power of saying whatever can be said, or what is appropriate to the occasion. This is what, in the speeches in tragedy, falls under the arts of politics and rhetoric; for the older poets make their personages discourse like statesmen, and the moderns like rhetoricians. One must not confuse it with character. Character in a play is that which reveals the moral purpose of the agents, i.e. the sort of thing they seek or avoid, where that is not obvious – hence there is no room for character in a speech on a purely indifferent subject. Thought, on the other hand, is shown in all they say when proving or disproving some particular point, or enunciating some universal proposition. Fourth among the literary elements is the diction of the personages, i.e. as before explained, the expression of their thoughts in words, which is practically the same thing with verse as with prose. As for the two remaining parts, the melody is the greatest of the pleasurable accessories of tragedy. The spectacle, though an attraction, is the least artistic of all the parts, and has least to do with the art of poetry. The tragic effect is quite possible without a public performance and actors; and besides, the getting-up of the spectacle is more a matter for the costumier than the poet.

The perfect plot, accordingly, must have a single, and not (as some tell us) a double issue; the change in the hero's fortunes must be not from misery to happiness, but on the contrary from happiness to misery; and the cause of it must lie not in any depravity, but in some great error on his part . . .

The tragic fear and pity may be aroused by the spectacle; but they may also be aroused by the very structure and incidents of the play – which is the better way and shows the better poet. The plot in fact should be so framed that, even without seeing the things take place, he who simply hears the account of them shall be filled with horror and pity at the incidents; which is just the effect that the mere recital of the story in *Oedipus* would have on one. To produce the same effect by means of the spectacle is less artistic, and requires extraneous aid. Those, however, who make use of the spectacle to put before us that which is merely monstrous and not productive of fear, are wholly out of touch with tragedy; not every kind of pleasure should be required of a tragedy, but only its own proper pleasure.

The tragic pleasure is that of pity and fear, and the poet has to produce it by a work of imitation; it is clear, therefore, that the causes should be included in the incidents of the story.

Sir Philip Sidney
An Apology for Poetry (1595)

Sidney reflects English preoccupation with continental neo-classical theory, and, mindful of Puritan attacks on drama, he stresses moral purpose. The superficial absurdities of ignoring the rules of the unities of time and place make an easy target.

Our tragedies and comedies (not without cause cried out against), observing rules neither of honest civility nor of skilful poetry, excepting *Gorboduc* (again, I say, of those that I have seen), which notwithstanding, as it is full of stately speeches and well sounding phrases, climbing to the height of Seneca's style, and as full of notable morality, which it does most delightfully teach, and so obtain the very end of poesy, yet in truth it is very defectious in the circumstances, which grieves me, because it might not remain as an exact model of all tragedies. For it is faulty both in place and time, the two necessary companions of all corporal actions. For where the stage should always represent but one place, and the uttermost time presupposed in it should be, both by Aristotle's precept and common reason, but one day, there is both many days, and many places, inartificially imagined. But if it be so in *Gorboduc*, how much more in all the rest, where you shall have Asia of the one side, and Africa of the other, and so many

22

other kingdoms, that the player, when he comes in, must ever begin with telling where he is, or else the tale will not be conceived. Now we shall have three ladies walk to gather flowers and then we must believe the stage to be a garden. By and by we hear news of shipwreck in the same place, and then we are to blame if we accept it not for a rock. Upon the back of that comes out a hideous monster, with fire and smoke, and then the miserable beholders are bound to take it for a cave. While in the meantime two armies fly in, represented with four swords and bucklers, and then what hard heart will not receive it for a pitched field? Now, of time they are much more liberal, for ordinary it is that two young princes fall in love. After many traverses, she is got with child, delivered of a fair boy; he is lost, grows a man, falls in love, and is ready to get another child; and all this in two hours space: which, how absurd it is in sense, even sense may imagine, and art has taught, and all ancient examples justified, and, at this day, the ordinary players in Italy will not err in. Yet will some bring in an example of *Eunuchus* in Terence, that contains matter of two days, yet far short of twenty years. True it is, and so was it to be played in two days, and so fitted to the time it set forth. And though Plautus has in one place done amiss, let us hit with him, and not miss with him. But they will say, How then shall we set forth a story, which contains both many places and many times? And do they not know that a tragedy is tied to the laws of poesy, and not of history; not bound to follow the story, but, having liberty, either to feign a quite new matter, or to frame the history to the most tragical conveniency? Again, many things may be told which cannot be showed, if they know the differences betwixt reporting and representing. As, for example, I may speak (though I am here) of Peru, and in speech digress from that to the description of Calicut; but in action I cannot represent it without Pacelot's horse. And so was the manner the ancients took, by some Nuncius to recount things done in former time, or other place.

John Dryden
The Grounds of Criticism in Tragedy (1679)

John Dryden provides the best critical guide to the English version of neo-classicism derived from the then fashionable French critics René Le Bossu and and René Rapin. Although Dryden rehearses the familiar tenets of classical tragedy, he offers a sane recognition of the native creativity of Shakespeare's approach. He puts the popular restoration appeal of the romantic intrigue of Spanish plots in perspective, and is serious but not pedantic in his support of classical virtues. Jacobean tragi-comedies had been popular, and comparing Shakespeare and Fletcher is apposite. Dryden's respect for classical theory, with its moral direction, is tempered by his reluctance to accept merely mechanical rules. He is aware of the Aristotelian mean, and his comments on the villainous character foreshadow critical perceptions of Iago. There is genuine admiration for Shakespeare's ability to portray human passions; but in his objections to Shakespeare's exuberant and fanciful use of language, Dryden voices the poetic prejudices of his own time. He recognizes the difficulty of reconciling classical theory with Shakespearean practice, but brings a writer's understanding to his appreciation of Shakespearean tragedy.

Tragedy is thus defined by Aristotle (omitting what I thought unnecessary in his definition). It is an imitation of one entire, great and probable action; not told, but represented; which, by moving in us fear and pity, is conducive to the purging of those two passions in our minds. More largely thus: tragedy describes or paints an action, which action must have all the properties above named. First, it must be one or single; that is, it must not be a history of one man's life, suppose of Alexander the Great, or Julius Caesar, but one single action of theirs. This condemns all Shakespeare's historical plays, which are rather chronicles represented, than tragedies; and all double action of plays. . . . The natural reason of this rule is plain; for two different independent actions distract the attention and concernment of the audience, and consequently destroy the intention of the poet; if his business be to move terror and pity, and one of his actions be comical, the other tragical, the former will divert the people, and utterly make void his greater purpose. Therefore, as in perspective, so in tragedy, here must be a point of sight in which all the lines terminate; otherwise the eye wanders, and the work is false. This was the practice of the Grecian stage. But Terence made an innovation in the Roman: all his plays have double actions; for it was his custom to translate two Greek comedies, and to weave them into one of his, yet so that both their actions were comical, and one was principal, the other but secondary or subservient. And this has obtained on the English stage, to give us the pleasure of variety.

As the action ought to be one, it ought, as such, to have order in it;

that is, to have a natural beginning, a middle, and an end. A natural beginning, says Aristotle, is that which could not necessarily have been placed after another thing; and so of the rest. This consideration will arraign all plays after the new model of Spanish plots, where accident is heaped upon accident, and that which is first might as reasonably be last; an inconvenience not to be remedied, but by making one accident naturally produce another, otherwise it is a farce and not a play . . .

The following properties of the action are so easy that they need not my explaining. It ought to be great, and to consist of great persons, to distinguish it from comedy, where the action is trivial, and the persons of inferior rank. The last quality of the action is, that it ought to be probable, as well as admirable and great . . .

To instruct delightfully is the general end of all poetry. Philosophy instructs, but it performs its work by precepts; which is not delightful, or not so delightful as example. To purge the passions by example is therefore the particular instruction which belongs to tragedy. Rapin, a judicious critic, has observed from Aristotle, that pride and want of commiseration are the most predominant vices of mankind; therefore, to cure us of these two, the inventors of tragedy have chosen to work upon two other passions, which are fear and pity . . .

After all, if any one will ask me whether a tragedy cannot be made upon any other grounds than those of exciting pity and terror in us, Bossu, the best of modern critics, answers thus in general: that all excellent arts, and particularly that of poetry, have been invented and brought to perfection by men of transcendent genius; and that, therefore, they who practise afterwards the same arts are obliged to tread in their footsteps, and to search in their writings the foundation of them; for it is not just that new rules should destroy the authority of the old. But Rapin writes more particularly thus, that no passions in a story are so proper to move our concernment as fear and pity; and that it is from our concernment we receive our pleasure is undoubted; when the soul becomes agitated with fear for one character, or hope for another, then it is that we are pleased in tragedy, by the interest which we take in their adventures.

Here, therefore, the general answer may be given to the first question, how far we ought to imitate Shakespeare and Fletcher in their plots; namely, that we ought to follow them so far only as they have copied the excellencies of those who invented and brought to perfection dramatic poetry; those things only excepted which religion, custom of countries, idioms of languages, etc., have altered in the superstructures, but not in the foundation of the design.

How defective Shakespeare and Fletcher have been in all their plots Mr. Rymer has discovered in his criticisms: neither can we, who follow them, be excused from the same or greater errors; which are the more unpardonable in us because we want their beauties to countervail our faults . . .

The difference between Shakespeare and Fletcher in their plotting seems to be this; Shakespeare generally moves more terror and Fletcher more compassion: for the first had a more masculine, a bolder and more fiery genius; the second, a more soft and womanish. In the mechanic beauties of the plot, which are the observation of the three unities, time, place, and action, they are both deficient; but Shakespeare most . . .

After the plot, which is the foundation of the play, the next thing to which we ought to apply our judgment is the manners; for now the poet comes to work above the ground. The groundwork, indeed, is that which is most necessary, as that upon which depends the firmness of the whole fabric; yet it strikes not the eye so much as the beauties or imperfections of the manners, the thoughts and the expressions.

The first rule which Bossu prescribes to the writer of an heroic poem, and which holds too by the same reason in all dramatic poetry, is to make the moral of the work; that is, to lay down to yourself what that precept of morality shall be which you would insinuate into the people . . . 'Tis the moral that directs the whole action of the play to one centre; and that action or fable is the example built upon the moral, which confirms the truth of it to our experience: when the fable is designed, then, and not before, the persons are to be introduced, with their manners, characters, and passions.

The manners in a poem are understood to be those inclinations, whether natural or acquired, which move and carry us to actions, good, bad, or indifferent, in a play; or which incline the persons to such or such actions. I have anticipated part of this discourse already in declaring that a poet ought not to make the manners perfectly good in his best persons; but neither are they to be more wicked in any of his characters than necessity requires. To produce a villain, without other reason than a natural inclination to villainy, is, in poetry, to produce an effect without a cause; and to make him more a villain than he has just reason to be is to make an effect which is stronger than the cause . . .

'Tis one of the excellencies of Shakespeare that the manners of his persons are generally apparent, and you see their bent and inclinations. Fletcher comes far short of him in this, as indeed he does in almost everything: there are but glimmerings of manners in most of his comedies, which run upon adventures; and many others of his best, are but pictures shown to you in the twilight; you know not whether they resemble vice or virtue, and they are either good, bad, or indifferent, as the present scene requires it. But of all poets, this commendation is to be given to Ben Jonson, that the manners even of the most inconsiderable persons in his plays are everywhere apparent.

To return once more to Shakespeare; no man ever drew so many characters, or generally distinguished 'em better from one another, excepting only Jonson. I will instance but in one to show the copiousness of his intention; it is that of Caliban, or the monster, in the *Tempest*. He seems there to have created a person which is not in nature, a boldness which, at first sight, would appear intolerable; for he makes him a species of himself, begotten by an incubus on a witch; but this, as I have elsewhere proved, is not wholly beyond the bounds of credibility, at least the vulgar still believe it. We have the separated notions of a spirit and of a witch (and spirits, according to Plato, are vested with a subtle body; according to some of his followers have different sexes); therefore, as from the distinct apprehensions of a horse and of a man imagination has formed a centaur, so from those of an incubus and a sorceress Shakespeare has produced his monster. Whether or no his generation can be defended I leave to philosophy; but of this I am certain, that the poet has most judiciously furnished him with a person, a language, and a character, which will suit him, both by father's and mother's side: he has all the discontents and malice of a witch and of a devil, besides a convenient portion of the deadly sins; gluttony, sloth, and lust are manifest; the dejectedness of a slave is likewise given him, and the ignorance of one bred up in a desert island. His person is monstrous, and he is the product of unnatural lust; and his language is as hobgoblin as his person; in all things he is distinguished from other mortals. The characters of Fletcher are poor and narrow in comparison of Shakespeare's; I remember not one which is not borrowed from him, unless you will accept that strange mixture of a man in the *King and No King*; so that in this part Shakespeare is generally worth our imitation, and to imitate Fletcher is but to copy after him who was a copyer . . .

If Shakespeare is allowed, as I think he must, to have made his characters distinct, it will easily be inferred that he understood the nature of the passions: because it has been proved already that confused passions make undistinguishable characters: yet I cannot deny that he has failings; but they are not so much in the passions themselves as in his manner of expression: he often obscures his meaning by his words, and sometimes makes it unintelligible. I will not say of so great a poet that he distinguished not the blown puffy style from true sublimity; but I may venture to maintain that the fury of his fancy often transported him beyond the bounds of judgment, either in coining of new words and phrases, or racking words which were in use into the violence of catachresis. It is not that I would explode the use of metaphors from passion, for Longinus thinks 'em necessary to raise it: but to use 'em at every work, to say nothing without a metaphor, a simile, an image, or description, is, I doubt, to smell a little too strongly of the buskin . . . But Shakespeare does not often thus; for the passions in his scene between Brutus and Cassius are extremely natural, the thoughts are such as arise from the matter, the expression of 'em not viciously figurative . . .

If Shakespeare were stripped of all the bombasts in his passions, and dressed in the most vulgar words, we should find the beauties of his thoughts remaining; if his embroideries were burnt down, there would still be silver at the bottom of the melting pot: but I fear (at least let me fear it for myself) that we, who ape his sounding words, have nothing of his thought, but are all outside; there is not so much as a dwarf within our giant's clothes. Therefore, let not Shakespeare suffer for our sakes; 'tis our fault, who succeed him in an age which is more refined, if we imitate him so ill that we copy his failing only and make a virtue of that in our writings which in his was an imperfection.

For what remains, the excellency of that poet was, as I have said, in the more manly passions; Fletcher's in the softer: Shakespeare writ betwixt man and man; Fletcher betwixt man and woman: consequently, the one described friendship better; the other love: yet Shakespeare taught Fletcher to write love: and Juliet and Desdemona are originals. 'Tis true the scholar had the softer soul; but the master had the kinder. Friendship is both a virtue and a passion essentially; love is a passion only in its nature, and it is not a virtue but by accident: good nature makes friendship; but effeminacy love. Shakespeare had a universal mind, which comprehended all characters and passions; Fletcher a more confined and limited: for though he treated love in perfection, yet honour, ambition, revenge, and generally all the stronger passions, he either touched not, or not masterly. To conclude all, he was a limb of Shakespeare.

Charles Gildon
An Essay on the Art, Rise, and Progress of the Stage in Greece, Rome and England (1710)

Charles Gildon's critical essays were published as a prefix to Nicholas Rowe's edition of Shakespeare's complete works. He is, therefore, an early critical commentator on the whole canon of the plays. Gildon takes issue with the exaggerated neo-classical attack of Rymer, but acknowledges that Shakespeare's achievement would have been greater if he had possessed a better knowledge of the ancients. For all that, Gildon does not accept the Romantic view that Shakespeare's natural genius flourished in complete ignorance of Latin and Greek. Like Dryden, Gildon takes a moderate stance, without glossing over the validity of the classical rules in relation to tragedy. He praises Shakespeare's depiction of manners through character and dialogue, giving futher currency to a persistent critical theme. In his view, departure from the rules is a blemish attributable to the age, but the truth at the heart of the tragedies cannot be obscured by pedantry.

'Tis my opinion that if Shakespeare had had those advantages of learning which the perfect knowledge of the ancients would have given him, so great a genius as his would have made him a very dangerous rival in fame of the greatest poets of antiquity, so far am I from seeing how this knowledge could either have curbed, confined, or spoiled the natural excellence of his writings. For though I must always think our author a miracle for the age he lived in yet I am obliged, in justice to reason and art, to confess that he does not come up to the ancients in all the beauties of the drama. But it is no small honour to him that he has surpassed them in the topics or common places . . .

It must be owned that Mr. Rymer carried the matter too far, since no man that has the least relish of poetry can question his genius. For in spite of his known and visible errors, when I read Shakespeare, even in some of his most irregular plays, I am surprised into a pleasure so great that my judgment is no longer free to see the faults, though they are never so great and evident. There is such a witchery in him that all the rules of art which he does not observe, though built on an equally solid and infallible reason, vanish away in the transports of those that he does observe, so entirely as if I had never known any thing of the matter. The pleasure, I confess, is peculiar as strong, for it comes from the admirable draughts of the manners visible in the distinction of his characters, and his surprizing reflections and topics, which are often extremely heightened by the expression and harmony of numbers; for in these no man ever excelled him and very few ever came up to his merit. Nor is his nice touching of the passion of joy the least source of this satisfaction, for he frequently moves this, in some of the most indifferent of his plays, so strongly that it is impossible to quell the emotion . . . The characters he has in his plays drawn of the Romans is a proof that he was acquainted with their historians, and Ben [Jonson] himself, in his Commendatory Verses before the first Folio Edition of Shakespeare's Works, allows him to have a little Latin and less Greek. That is, he would not allow him to be as perfect a critic in the Latin as he himself was, but yet that he was capable of reading at least the Latin poets – as is, I think, plainly proved. For I can see no manner of weight in that conjecture which supposes that he never read the ancients because he has not any where imitated them, so fertile a genius as his having no need to borrow images from others which had such plenty of his own. Besides, we find by experience that some of our modern authors, nay those who have made great figures in the university for their wit and learning, have so little followed the ancients in their performances that by them a man could never guess that they had read a word of them, and yet they would take it amiss not to be allowed to be very well read in both Latin and Greek poets. If they do this in their writings out of pride or want of capacity, may we not as justly suppose that Shakespeare did it out of an abundance in his own natural stock? I contend not here to prove that he was a perfect master of either the Latin or Greek authors, but all that I aim is to show that as he was capable of reading some of the Romans so he had actually read Ovid and Plautus without spoiling or confining his fancy or genius.

Whether his ignorance of the ancients were a disadvantage to him or no, may admit of a dispute . . .

Nature enabled Shakespeare to succeed in the manners and diction often to perfection, but he could never by his force and genius or nature vanquish the barbarous mode of the times and come to any excellence in the fable, except in the *Merry Wives of Windsor* and the *Tempest*.

Next to the fable the manners are the most considerable (and in these Shakespeare has generally excelled, as will be seen when we come to his plays). For as tragedy is the imitation of an action so there are no actions without the manners, since the manners are the cause of the actions. By the manners we discover the inclinations of the speaker, what part, side, or course he will take on any important and difficult emergence, and know how he will behave himself before we see his actions. Thus we know from the manners of Achilles what answer he will give the ambassadors of Agamemnon by what the poet has told us of his hero. And when Mercury brings Jove's orders to Aeneas we know that the piety of the hero will prevail over love. And the character of Oedipus makes us expect his extravagant passions and the excesses he will commit by his obstinacy. Those discourses therefore that do not do this are without manners. The character of Coriolanus in Shakespeare prepares us to expect the resolution he will take to disoblige the people, for pride naturally contemns inferiors and over-values itself. The same may be said of Tybalt in *Romeo and Juliet*, and most of the characters of this poet.

The sentiments are the next in degree of excellence to the fable and the manners, and justly demand the third place in our care and study, for those are for the manners as the manners for the subject fable. The action can't be justly imitated without the manners, nor the manners expressed without the sentiments. In these we must regard truth and verisimilitude, as when the poet makes the madman speak exactly as a madman does, or as 'tis probable he would do. This Shakespeare has admirably performed in the madness of King Lear, where the cause of his frenzy is ever uppermost and mingles with all he says or does . . .

For to make a good tragedy, that is, a just imitation, the action imitated ought not in reality to be longer than the representation; for by that means it has the more likeness and by consequence is the most perfect. But as there are actions of ten or twelve hours, and the representations cannot possibly be so long, then we must bring in some of the incidents in the intervals of the acts the better to deceive the audience, who cannot be imposed on with such tedious and long actions as we have generally on the stage, as whole lives, and many actions of the same man, where the probable is lost as well as the necessary. And in this our Shakespeare is every where faulty through the ignorant mode of the age in which he lived, and which I instance not as a reproach to his memory but only to warn the reader or young poet to avoid the same error.

William Guthrie
An Essay upon English Tragedy (1747)

William Guthrie answers a neo-classical attack on Shakespeare's tragedies by Jean-Bernard Le Blanc. He opposes the enduring popularity of the plays to the pedantries of classicism, and signifies a critical trend in stressing the variety of Shakespearean characterization.

Where is the Briton so much of a Frenchman as to prefer the highest stretch of modern improvements to the meanest spark of Shakespeare's genius? Yet to our eternal amazement it is true, that for above half a century the poets and the patrons of poetry in England abandoned the sterling merit of Shakespeare for the tinsel ornaments of the French Academy. Let us observe, however, to the honour of our country, that neither the practice of her poets nor the example of their patrons could extinguish in the minds of the people their love of their darling writer. His scenes were still admired, his passions were ever felt; his powerful nature knocked at the breast; fashion could not stifle affection; the British spirit at length prevailed; wits with their patrons were forced to give way to genius; and the plays of Shakespeare are now as much crowded as, perhaps, they were in the days of their author.

Nothing has contributed more to the reproachful, the ignominious fashion of neglecting Shakespeare's manner than the not understanding aright the character of that pride of human genius. A young gentleman naturally of a fine turn for letters goes to the university, where the amusements of wit mingle with, nay often lead, his other studies, and one of the first things his tutor tells him is that all poetry is or ought to be an imitation of nature; and he confirms this doctrine by a number of passages from poets ancient and modern. This agrees perfectly well with all the flimsy French dissertations, or English ones stolen from the French, which fall into his pupil's hands upon subjects of delicacy, taste, correctness, AND ALL THAT. When his head is quite warm with their notions and when he imagines his taste, or something which he takes to be taste, is entirely formed he applies his rules to Shakespeare, and finds many of them not answer. He is soon after turned over to a Swiss or a Scotsman, who LEADS him to travel;

and in France he has all his notions of delicacy confirmed and rivetted. He returns to England, where he hears the praises of Shakespeare with silent contempt; he tacitly pities every man who loves so unnatural an author, and bursts for an opportunity to discharge his spleen among his French and foreign acquaintances.

In reality the gentleman is not to be blamed. He proceeds upon a maxim which, however true when applied to most other writers, fails in Shakespeare.

Shall I attempt to give the reason of this? It is not Shakespeare who speaks the language of nature, but nature rather speaks the language of Shakespeare. He is not so much her imitator as her master, her director, her moulder. Nature is a stranger to objects which Shakespeare has rendered natural. Nature never created a Caliban till Shakespeare introduced the monster, and we now take him to be nature's composition. Nature never meant that the fairest, the gentlest, the most virtuous of her sex should fall in love with a rough, blustering, awkward Moor; she never meant that this Moor, in the course of a barbarous jealousy, and during the commission of a detestable murder, should be the chief object of compassion throughout the play. Yet Shakespeare has effected all this; and every sigh that rises, every tear that drops, is prompted by nature.

Nature never designed that a complication of the meanest, the most infamous, the most execrable qualities should form so agreeable a composition, that we think Henry the fifth makes a conquest of himself when he discards Jack Falstaff. Yet Shakespeare has struck out this moral contradiction, and reconciled it to nature. There is not a spectator who does not wish to drink a cup of sack with the merry mortal, and who does not in his humour forget, nay sometimes love his vices.

Give me leave further to observe that beauties have, in Homer and other authors, been magnified into miracles which, without being noted, are more perfect, more frequent, and better marked in Shakespeare than in Homer himself.

To what extravagance has that father of ancient poetry been justly raised for making so many of his heroes extremely brave, yet assigning to each a different character of courage! But to what perfection has our heaven-instructed Englishman brought this excellency which the French critics are so proud of having discovered in Homer? He has not confined it to courage but carried it through every quality. His fools are as different from one another as his heroes. But above all, how has he varied guilty ambition in a species so narrow of itself, that it seems impossible to diversify it! For see Hamlet's father-in-law, Macbeth, King John, and King Richard, all rising to royalty by murdering their kindred kings. Yet what a character has Shakespeare affixed to every instance of the same species. Observe the remorse of the Dane, how varied it is from the distraction of the Scot: mark the confusion of John, how different from both; while the close, the vigilant, the jealous guilt of Richard is peculiar to himself.

Samuel Johnson
Preface to *The Plays of William Shakespeare* (1765)

Dr Johnson was not the first to question the pedantic application of neo-classical rules to Shakespeare, but the high style of this famous preface ensured its lasting authority. Johnson alternates between critical attacks on Shakespeare for failing to stress the moral purpose of his characters and themes, and fulsome praise which searches for the memorable sentence in generalized statements. Although Johnson was prepared to take a liberal view of the mingling of tragedy and comedy, his critical denigration of Shakespearean tragedy resounds with the prejudices of his time. However liberal his protestation about the rules of the unities, Johnson laments Shakespeare's lack of classical decorum and sense of overall control. His singular labelling of Shakespeare's habitual indulgence in quibbles as 'the fatal Cleopatra' was to be frequently quoted in critical arguments over the language of the plays. The analysis of the neo-classical view was to help toward a common-sense approach to the unities, but it is clear that Johnson's critical stance is based on the textual tradition of classical literary studies.

Shakespeare engaged in dramatic poetry with the world open before him; the rules of the ancients were yet known to few; the public judgment was unformed; he had no example of such fame as might force him upon imitation, nor critics of such authority as might restrain his extravagance. He therefore indulged his natural disposition, and his disposition, as Rymer has remarked, led him to comedy. In tragedy he often writes with great appearance of toil and study, what is written at last with little felicity; but in his comic scenes he seems to produce without labour what no labour can improve. In tragedy he is always struggling after some occasion to be comic, but in comedy he seems to repose, or to luxuriate, as in a mode of thinking congenial to his nature. In his tragic scenes there is always something wanting, but his comedy often surpasses expectation or desire. His comedy pleases by the thoughts and the language, and his tragedy for the greater part by incident and action. His tragedy seems to be skill, his comedy to be instinct.

The force of his comic scenes has suffered little diminution from the changes made by a century and a half, in manners or in words. As his personages act upon principles arising from genuine passion, very little modified by particular forms, their pleasures and vexations are communicable to all times and to all places; they are natural, and therefore durable; the adventitious peculiarities of personal habits are only superficial dyes, bright and pleasing for a little while, yet soon fading to a dim tinct without any remains of former lustre; but the discriminations of true passion are the colours of nature; they pervade the whole mass, and can only perish with the body that exhibits them. The accidental composition of heteregeneous modes are dissolved by the chance which combined them; but the uniform simplicity of primitive qualities neither admits increase nor suffers decay. The sand heaped by one flood is scattered by another, but the rock always continues in its place. The stream of time, which is continually washing the dissoluble fabrics of other poets, passes without injury by the adamant of Shakespeare . . .

Shakespeare's familiar dialogue is affirmed to be smooth and clear, yet not wholly without ruggedness or difficulty; as a country may be eminently fruitful, though it has spots unfit for cultivation. His characters are praised as natural though their sentiments are sometimes forced, and their actions improbable; as the earth upon the whole is spherical, though its surface is varied with protuberances and cavities.

Shakespeare with his excellencies has likewise his faults, and faults sufficient to obscure and overwhelm any other merit. I shall shew them in the proportion in which they appear to me, without envious malignity or superstitious veneration. No question can be more innocently discussed than a dead poet's pretensions to renown; and little regard is due to that bigotry which sets candour higher than truth.

His first defect is that to which may be imputed most of the evil in books or in men. He sacrifices virtue to convenience, and is so much more careful to please than to instruct that he seems to write without any moral purpose. From his writings indeed a system of social duty may be selected, for he that thinks reasonably must think morally; but his precepts and axioms drop casually from him; he makes no just distribution of good or evil, nor is always careful to shew in the virtuous a disapprobation of the wicked; he carries his persons indifferently through right and wrong, and at the close dismisses them without further care, and leaves their example to operate by chance. This fault the barbarity of his age cannot extenuate; for it is always a writer's duty to make the world better, and justice is a virtue independent of time or place.

The plots are often so loosely formed that a very slight consideration may improve them, and so carelessly pursued that he seems not always fully to comprehend his own design. He omits opportunities of instructing or delighting which the train of his story seems to force upon him, and apparently rejects those exhibitions which would be more affecting for the sake of those which are more easy.

It may be observed that in many of his plays the latter part is evidently neglected. When he found himself near the end of his work, and in view of his reward, he shortened the labour to snatch the profit. He therefore remits his efforts where he should most vigorously exert them, and his catastrophe is improbably produced or imperfectly represented.

He had no regard to distinction of time or place, but gives to one age or nation, without scruple, the customs, institutions, and opinions of another, at the expense not only of likelihood but of possibility . . .

In tragedy his performance seems constantly to be worse, as his labour is more. The effusions of passion which exigence forces out are for the most part striking and energetic; but whenever he solicits his invention, or strains his faculties, the offspring of his throes is tumour, meanness, tediousness, and obscurity.

In narration he affects a disproportionate pomp of diction and a wearisome train of circumlocution, and tells the incident imperfectly in many words, which might have been more plainly delivered in few. Narration in dramatic poetry is naturally tedious, as it is unanimated and inactive, and obstructs the progress of the action; it should therefore always be rapid, and enlivened by frequent interruption. Shakespeare found it an encumbrance, and instead of lightening it by brevity endeavoured to recommend it by dignity and splendour.

His declamations or set speeches are commonly cold and weak, for his power was the power of nature; when he endeavoured, like other tragic writers, to catch opportunities of amplification, and instead of enquiring what the occasion demanded, to show how much his stores of knowledge could supply, he seldom escapes without the pity or resentment of his reader.

It is incident to him to be now and then entangled with an unwieldy sentiment, which he cannot well express, and will not reject; he struggles with it a while, and if it continues stubborn comprises it in words such as occur, and leaves it to be disentangled and evolved by those who have more leisure to bestow upon it.

Not that always where the language is intricate the thought is subtle, or the image always great where the line is bulky; the equality of words to things is very often neglected, and trivial sentiments and vulgar ideas disappoint the attention, to which they are recommended by sonorous epithets and swelling figures.

But the admirers of this great poet have never the less reason to indulge their hopes of supreme excellence than when he seems fully resolved to sink them in dejection, and mollify them with tender emotions by the fall of greatness, the danger of innocence, or the crosses of love. He is not long soft and pathetic without some idle conceit, or contemptible equivocation. He no sooner begins to move than he counteracts himself; and terror and pity, as they are rising in the mind, are checked and blasted by sudden frigidity.

A quibble is to Shakespeare what luminous vapours are to the traveller; he follows it at all adventures, it is sure to lead him out of his way, and sure to engulf him in the mire. It has some malignant power over his mind, and its fascinations are irresistible. Whatever be the dignity or profundity of his disquisition, whether he be enlarging knowledge or exalting affection, whether he be amusing attention with incidents or enchaining it in suspense, let but a quibble spring up before him and he leaves his work unfinished. A quibble is the golden apple for which he will always turn aside from his career, or stoop from his elevation. A quibble, poor and barren as it is, gave him such delight that he was content to purchase it by the sacrifice of reason, propriety and truth. A quibble was to him the fatal Cleopatra for which he lost the world, and was content to lose it.

It will be thought strange that, in enumerating the defects of this writer, I have not yet mentioned his neglect of the unities, his violation of those laws which have been instituted and established by the joint authority of poets and critics.

For his other deviations from the art of writing I resign him to critical justice, without making any other demand in his favour than that which must be indulged to all human excellence, that his virtues be rated with his failings. But from the censure which this irregularity may bring upon him I shall, with due reverence to that learning which I must oppose, adventure to try how I can defend him.

His histories, being neither tragedies nor comedies, are not subject to any of their laws; nothing more is necessary to all the praise which they expect than that the changes of action be so prepared as to be understood, that the incidents be various and affecting, and the characters consistent, natural and distinct. No other unity is intended, and therefore none is to be sought.

In his other works he has well enough preserved the unity of action. He has not, indeed, an intrigue regularly perplexed and regularly unravelled; he does not endeavour to hide his design only to discover it, for this is seldom the order of real events, and Shakespeare is the poet of nature. But his plan has commonly what Aristotle requires, a beginning, a middle, and an end; one event is concatenated with another and the conclusion follows by easy consequences. There are perhaps some incidents that might be spared, as in other poets there is much talk that only fills up time upon the stage; but the general system makes gradual advances, and the end of the play is the end of expectation.

To the unities of time and place he has shewn no regard, and perhaps a nearer view of the principles on which they stand will diminish their value, and withdraw them from the veneration which from the time of Corneille they have very generally received, by discovering that they have given more trouble to the poet than pleasure to the auditor.

The necessity of observing the unities of time and place arises from the supposed necessity of making the drama credible. The critics hold it impossible that an action of months or years can be possibly believed to pass in three hours; or that the spectator can suppose himself to sit in the theatre while ambassadors go and return between distant kings, while armies are levied and towns besieged, while an exile wanders and returns, or till he whom they saw courting his mistress shall lament the untimely fall of his son. The mind revolts from evident falsehood, and fiction loses its force when it departs from the resemblance of reality.

From the narrow limitations of time necessarily arises the contraction of place. The spectator who knows that he saw the first act at Alexandria cannot suppose that he sees the next at Rome, at a distance to which not the dragons of Medea could in so short a time have transported him; he knows with certainty that he had not changed his place; and he knows that place cannot change itself, that what was a house cannot become a plain, that what was Thebes can never be Persepolis.

Such is the triumphant language with which a critic exults over the misery of an irregular poet, and exults commonly without resistance or reply. It is time therefore to tell him, by the authority of Shakespeare, that he assumes as an unquestionable principle a position which, while his breath is forming into words, his understanding pronounces to be false. It is false that any representation is mistaken for reality; that any dramatic fable in its materiality was ever credible, or, for a single moment, was ever credited . . .

The truth is, that the spectators are always in their senses, and know from the first act to the last that the stage is only a stage, and that the players are only players. They come to hear a certain number of lines recited with just gesture and elegant modulation. The lines relate to some action, and an action must be in some place; but the different actions that complete a story may be in places very remote from each other; and where is the absurdity of allowing that space to represent first Athens and then Sicily, which was always known to be neither Sicily nor Athens, but a modern theatre?

By supposition, as place is introduced, time may be extended; the time required by the fable elapses for the most part between the acts; for, of so much of the action as is represented, the real and poetical duration is the same. If, in the first act, preparations for war against Mithridates are represented to be made in Rome, the event of the war may, without absurdity, be represented in the catastrophe, as happening in Pontus; we know that there is neither war, nor preparation for war; we know that we are neither in Rome nor Pontus; that neither Mithridates nor Lucullus are before us. The drama exhibits successive imitations of successive actions, and why may not the second imitation represent an action that happened years after the first, if it be so connected with it that nothing but time can be supposed to intervene? Time is, of all modes of existence, most obsequious to the imagination; a lapse of years is as easily conceived as a passage of hours. In contemplation we easily contract the time of real actions, and therefore willingly permit it to be contracted when we only see their imitation.

It will be asked how the drama moves, if it is not credited. It is credited with all the credit due to drama. It is credited, whenever it moves, as a just picture of a real original; as representing to the auditor what he would himself feel, if he were to do or suffer what is there feigned to be suffered or to be done. The reflection that strikes the heart is not that the evils before us are real evils, but that they are evils to which we ourselves may be exposed. If there be any fallacy, it is not that we fancy the players, but that we fancy ourselves unhappy for a moment; but we rather lament the possibility than suppose the presence of misery, as a mother weeps over her babe when she remembers that death may take it from her. The delight of tragedy proceeds from our consciousness of fiction; if we thought murders and treasons real they would please no more.

Imitations produce pain or pleasure not because they are mistaken for realities but because they bring realities to mind. When the imagination is recreated by a painted landscape, the trees are not supposed capable to give us shade or the fountains coolness; but we consider how we should be pleased with such fountains playing beside us, and such woods waving over us. We are agitated in reading the history of Henry the Fifth, yet no man takes his book for the field of Agincourt. A dramatic exhibition is a book recited with concomitants that increase or diminish its effect. Familiar comedy is often more powerful in the theatre than on the page; imperial tragedy is always less. The humour of Petruchio may be heightened by grimace, but what voice or what gesture can hope to add dignity to the soliloquy of Cato?

A play read affects the mind like a play acted. It is therefore evident that the action is not supposed to be real, and it follows that between the acts a longer or shorter time may be allowed to pass, and that no more account of space or duration is to be taken by the auditor of a drama than by the reader of a narrative, before whom may pass in an hour the life of a hero or the revolutions of an empire.

Whether Shakespeare knew the unities, and rejected them by design, or deviated from them by happy ignorance it is, I think, impossible to decide, and useless to inquire. We may reasonably suppose that when he rose to notice he did not want the counsels and admonitions of scholars and critics, and that he at last deliberately persisted in a practice which he might have begun by chance. As nothing is essential to the fable but unity of action, and as the unities of time and place arise evidently from false assumptions, and by circumscribing the extent of the drama lessen its variety, I cannot think it much to be lamented that they were not known by him, or not observed.

Thomas Whately
Remarks on Some of the Characters of Shakespeare
(1785)

This fragment of a study comparing the characters of Richard III and

Macbeth was praised by Horace Walpole but criticized by others for its interpretation of the moral significance of Macbeth. *Whately represents the move towards character study in place of arid discussion of the unities.*

The writers upon dramatic composition have, for the most part, confined their observations to the fable; and the maxims received amongst them, for the conduct of it, are therefore emphatically called the *Rules of the Drama.* It has been found easy to give and to apply them; they are obvious, they are certain, they are general; and poets without genius have by observing them pretended to fame; while critics without discernment have assumed importance from knowing them. But the regularity thereby established, though highly proper, is by no means the first requisite in a dramatic composition. Even waiving all consideration of those finer feelings which a poet's imagination or sensibility imparts, there is within the colder provinces of judgment and of knowledge a subject for criticism more worthy of attention than the common topics of discussion. I mean the distinction and preservation of *character*, without which the piece is at best a tale, not an action; for the actors in it are not produced upon the scene. They were distinguished by character; all men are; by that we know them, by that we are interested in their fortunes; by that their conduct, their sentiments, their very language is formed: and whenever, therefore, the proper marks of it are missing we immediately perceive that the person before our eyes is but suppositious. Experience has shown that however rigidly, and however rightly, the unities of action, time, and place have been insisted on, they may be dispensed with, and the magic of the scene may make the absurdity invisible. Most of Shakespeare's plays abound with instances of such a fascination . . .

Yet the generality of dramatic writers, and more especially of those who have chosen tragedy for their subject, have contented themselves with the distant resemblance which indiscriminate expressions of passion, and imperfect, because general, marks of character can give. Elevated ideas become the hero; a professed contempt of all principles denotes a villain; frequent gusts of rage betray a violence, and tender sentiments shew a mildness of disposition. But a villain differs not more from a saint than he does in some particulars from another as bad as himself; and the same degrees of anger, excited by the same occasions, break forth in as many several shapes as there are various tempers. But these distinguishing peculiarities between man and man have too often escaped the observation of tragic writers. The comic writers have indeed frequently caught them; but then they are apt to fall into an excess the other way, and overcharge their imitations.

Shakespeare has generally avoided both extremes; and however faulty in some respects is in this, the most essential part of the drama, considered as a representation, excellent beyond comparison. No other dramatic writer could ever pretend to so deep and so extensive a knowledge of the human heart; and he had a genius to express all that his penetration could discover. The characters, therefore, which he has drawn are masterly copies from nature; differing each from the other, and animated as the originals though correct to a scrupulous precision. The truth and force of the imitation recommend it as a subject worthy of criticism . . .

Every play of Shakespeare abounds with instances of his excellence in distinguishing characters. It would be difficult to determine which is the most striking of all that he drew; but his merit will appear most conspicuously by comparing two opposite characters, who happened to be placed in similar circumstances. Not that on such occasions he marks them more strongly than on others, but because the contrast makes the distinction more apparent; and of these none seem to agree so much in situation, and to differ so much in disposition, as RICHARD THE THIRD and MACBETH. Both are soldiers, both usurpers; both attain the throne by the same means, by treason and murder; and both lose it too in the same manner, in battle against the person claiming it as lawful heir. Perfidy, violence, and tyranny are common to both; and those only, their obvious qualities, would have been attributed indiscriminately to both by an ordinary dramatic writer. But Shakespeare, in conformity to the truth of history as far as it led him, and by improving upon the fables which have been blended with it, has ascribed opposite principles and motives to the same designs and actions, and various effects to the operation of the same events upon different tempers. Richard and Macbeth, as represented by him, agree in nothing but their fortunes.

Maurice Morgann
'An Essay on the Dramatic Character of
Sir John Falstaff' (1777)

Morgann's detailed vindication of Falstaff from the charge of cowardice has long been regarded as a landmark in Shakespearean

criticism. Exemplifying the trend in close character analysis, the essay
includes a general recognition of Shakespeare's distinctive power of
character portrayal. There is more than a dismissal of pedantic rules
from the appreciation of Shakespeare, for Morgann distinguishes the
life-like fascination of the characters. This hint at the living indepen-
dence of Shakespeare's characters, beyond their appearance in the
context of the plays, was to be exaggerated in later critical approaches.

Shakespeare is a name so interesting, that it is excusable to stop a
moment, nay it would be indecent to pass him without the tribute of
some admiration. He differs essentially from all other writers; him we
may profess rather to feel than to understand; and it is safer to say, on
many occasions, that we are possessed by him, than that we possess
him. And no wonder; he scatters the seeds of things, the principles of
character and action, with so cunning a hand yet with so careless an
air, and, master of our feelings, submits himself so little to our
judgment, that everything seems superior. We discern not his course,
we see no connection of cause and effect, we are rapt in ignorant
admiration, and claim no kindred with his abilities. All the incidents,
all the parts, look like chance, whilst we feel and are sensible that the
whole is design. His characters not only act and speak in strict
conformity to nature, but in strict relation to us; just so much is shewn
as is requisite, just so much is impressed; he commands every passage
to our heads and to our hearts, and moulds us as he pleases, and that
with so much ease, that he never betrays his own exertions. We see
these characters act from mingled motives of passion, reason, interest,
habit and complexion, in all their proportions, when they are
supposed to know it not themselves; and we are made to acknowledge
that their actions and sentiments are, from these motives, the
necessary result. He at once blends and distinguishes every thing;
every thing is complicated, every thing is plain. I restrain the further
expressions of my admiration lest they should not seem applicable to
man; but it is really astonishing that a mere human being, a part of
humanity only, should so perfectly comprehend the whole; and that
he should possess such exquisite art, that whilst every woman and
every child shall feel the whole effect, his learned editors and
commentators should yet so very frequently mistake or seem ignorant
of the cause. A sceptre or a straw are in his hands of equal efficacy; he
needs no selection; he converts every thing into excellence; nothing is
too great, nothing is too base. Is a character efficient like Richard, it is

every thing we can wish; is it otherwise, like Hamlet, it is productive of equal admiration: action produces one mode of excellence and inaction another: the chronicle, the novel, or the ballad; the king, or the beggar, the hero, the madman, the sot or the fool; it is all one; nothing is worse, nothing is better: the same genius pervades and is equally admirable in all. Or, is a character to be shewn in progressive change, and the events of years comprized within the hour; with what a magic hand does he prepare and scatter his spells! The understanding must, in the first place, be subdued; and lo! how the rooted prejudices of the child spring up to confound the man! The weird sisters rise, and order is extinguished. The laws of nature give way, and leave nothing in our minds but wildness and horror. No pause is allowed us for reflection: horrid sentiment, furious guilt, and inchantment, shake and *possess us wholly*. In the mean time the *process* is completed. *Macbeth* changes under our eye, *the milk of human kindness is converted to gall*; he has *supped full of horrors* and his *May of life is fallen into the sear, the yellow leaf*; whilst we, the fools of amazement are insensible to the shifting of place and the lapse of time, and till the curtain drops, never once wake to the truth of things, or recognize the laws of existence . . .

The reader must be sensible of something in the composition of Shakespeare's characters, which renders them essentially different from those drawn by other writers. The characters of every drama must indeed be grouped; but in the groups of other poets the parts which are not seen, do not in fact exist. But there is a certain roundness and integrity in the forms of Shakespeare, which give them an independence as well as a relation, insomuch that we often meet with passages, which though perfectly felt, cannot be sufficiently explained in words, without unfolding the whole character of the speaker.

Charles Lamb
On the Tragedies of Shakespeare (1811)

For Lamb Shakespeare's plays deserve the liberty of the imagination, not the restriction of popular theatricality. Romantic freedom accorded Shakespearean tragedy the same status as the greatest of the classics, and Lamb could not conceive the necessary intellectual and emotional involvement being possible in the theatrical interpretations of his day.

It may seem a paradox, but I cannot help being of opinion that the plays of Shakespeare are less calculated for performance on the stage, than those of almost any other dramatist whatever. Their distinguishing excellence is a reason that they should be so. There is so much in them, which comes not under the province of acting, with which eye, and tone, and gesture, have nothing to do.

The glory of the scenic art is to personate passion, and the turn of passion; and the more coarse and palpable the passion is, the more hold upon the eyes and ears of the spectators the performers obviously possess. For this reason, scolding scenes, scenes where two persons talk themselves into a fit of fury, and then in a surprising manner talk themselves out of it again, have always been the most popular upon our stage. And the reason is plain, because the spectators are here most palpably appealed to, they are the proper judges in this war of words, they are the legitimate ring that should be formed round such 'intellectual prize-fighters'. Talking is the direct object of the imitation here. But in all the best drama, and in Shakespeare above all, how obvious it is, that the form of *speaking*, whether it be in soliloquy or dialogue, is only a medium, and often a highly artificial one, for putting the reader or spectator into possession of that knowledge of the inner structure and workings of mind in a character, which he could otherwise never have arrived at *in that form of composition* by any gift short of intuition. We do here as we do with novels written in the *epistolary form*. How many improprieties, perfect solecisms in letter-writing, do we put up with in *Clarissa* and other books, for the sake of the delight which that form upon the whole gives us.

But the practice of stage representation reduces every thing to a controversy of elocution. Every character, from the boisterous blasphemings of Bajazeth to the shrinking timidity of womanhood, must play the orator. The love-dialogue of Romeo and Juliet, those silver-sweet sounds of lovers' tongues by night; the more intimate and sacred sweetness of nuptial colloquy between an Othello or a Posthumous with their married wives, all those delicacies which are so delightful in the reading, as when we read of those youthful dalliances in Paradise –

As beseem'd
Fair couple link'd in happy nuptial league,
Alone:

by the inherent fault of stage representation, how are these things sullied and turned from their very nature by being exposed to a large assembly; when such speeches as Imogen addresses to her lord, come drawling out of the mouth of a hired actress, whose courtship, though nominally addressed to the personated Posthumous, is manifestly aimed at the spectators, who are to judge of her endearments and her returns of love . . .

It requires little reflection to perceive, that if those characters in Shakespeare which are within the precincts of nature, have yet something in them which appeals too exclusively to the imagination, to admit of their being made objects to the senses without suffering a change and a diminution, – that still stronger the objection must lie against representing another line of characters, which Shakespeare has introduced to give a wildness and a supernatural elevation to his scenes, as if to remove them still further from that assimilation to common life in which their excellence is vulgarly supposed to consist. When we read the incantations of those terrible beings the Witches in *Macbeth*, though some of the ingredients of their hellish composition savour of the grotesque, yet is the effect upon us other than the most serious and appalling that can be imagined? Can any mirth accompany a sense of their presence? We might as well laugh under a consciousness of the principle of Evil himself being truly and really present with us. But attempt to bring these beings on to a stage, and you turn them instantly into so many old women, that men and children are to laugh at. Contrary to the old saying, that 'seeing is believing', the sight actually destroys the faith; and the mirth in which we indulge at their expense, when we see these creatures upon a stage, seems to be a sort of indemnification which we make to ourselves for the terror which they put us in when reading made them an object of belief, – when we surrendered up our reason to the poet, as children to their nurses and their elders; and we laugh at our fears, as children who thought they saw something in the dark, triumph when the bringing in of a candle discovers the vanity of their fears. For this exposure of supernatural agents upon a stage is truly bringing in a candle to expose their own delusiveness. It is the solitary taper and the book that generates a faith in these terrors: a ghost by chandelier light, and in good company, deceives no spectators, – a ghost that can be measured by the eye, and his human dimensions made out at leisure. The sight of a well-lighted house, and a well-dressed audience, shall arm the most nervous child against any apprehensions: as Tom Brown says of the impenetrable skin of Achilles with his impenetrable armour over it, 'Bully Dawson would have fought the devil with such advantages'. . . .

The reading of a tragedy is a fine abstraction. It presents to the fancy just so much of external appearances as to make us feel that we are among flesh and blood, while by far the greater and better part of our imagination is employed upon the thoughts and internal machinery of the character. But in acting, scenery, dress, the most contemptible things, call upon us to judge of their naturalness.

Perhaps it would be no bad similitude, to liken tne pleasure which we take in seeing one of these fine plays acted, compared with that quiet delight which we find in the reading of it, to the different feelings with which a reviewer, and a man that is not a reviewer, reads a fine poem. The accursed critical habit, – the being called upon to judge and pronounce, must make it quite a different thing to the former. In seeing these plays acted, we are affected just as judges. When Hamlet compares the two pictures of Gertrude's first and second husband, who wants to see the pictures? But in the acting, a miniature must be lugged out; which we know not to be the picture, but only to shew how finely a miniature may be represented. This shewing of everything, levels all things; it makes tricks, bows, and curtesies, of importance. Mrs. S never got more fame by any thing than by the manner in which she dismisses the guests in the banquet scene in *Macbeth*: it is as much remembered as any of her thrilling tones or impressive looks. But does such a trifle as this enter into the imaginations of the readers of that wild and wonderful scene? Does not the mind dismiss the feasters as rapidly as it can? Does it care about the gracefulness of the doing it? But by acting, and judging of acting, all these non-essentials are raised into an importance, injurious to the main interest of the play.

Samuel Taylor Coleridge
Biographia Literaria (1817)

In his major critical work Coleridge investigates the 'principles of writing' and places Shakespeare firmly in the great classical tradition where the creative energy of the poet incorporates the wisdom of philosophy. For Coleridge Shakespeare is neither the gifted barbarian nor the Renaissance pedant, but in his drama achieves the classical balance of creative power and intellectual energy.

No man was ever yet a great poet, without being at the same time a profound philosopher. For poetry is the blossom and the fragrancy of all human knowledge, human thoughts, human passions, emotions, language. In Shakespeare's poems the creative power and the intellectual energy wrestle as in a warlike embrace. Each in its excess of strength seems to threaten the extinction of the other. At length in the drama they were reconciled, and fought each with its shield before the breast of the other. Or like two rapid streams, that, at their first meeting within narrow and rocky banks, mutually strive to repel each other and intermix reluctantly and in tumult; but soon finding a wider channel and more yielding shores blend, and dilate, and flow on in one current and with one voice . . .

What then shall we say? even this; that Shakespeare, no mere child of nature; no *automaton* of genius; no passive vehicle of inspiration, possessed by the spirit, not possessing it; first studied patiently, meditated deeply, understood minutely, till knowledge, become habitual and intuitive, wedded itself to his habitual feelings, and at length gave birth to that stupendous power, by which he stands alone, with no equal or second in his own class; to that power which seated him on one of the two glory-smitten summits of the poetic mountain with Milton as his compeer not rival.

Lectures on Shakespeare (1818)

Coleridge applies an informed and comparative approach to classical and Shakespearean tragedy. He expresses the essence of Romanticism in its striving for the infinite, against the finite certainties of the Greeks with their overwhelming sense of a pre-determined fate. A reasoned case for treating Shakespearean tragedy as a distinctive genre is put forward by Coleridge, and he stresses the importance of the imagination, which was a central theme of his critical theories. On the subject of stage-illusion Coleridge offers a more positive assessment than Lamb's rejection of theatrical representation. In detailed comparison with classical form, Coleridge insists that Shakespearean tragedy had its own rationale, that it was not the expression of a lawless phenomenon, but an organic form controlled by Shakespeare's judgment.

The Greek tragedy may rather be compared to our serious opera than to the tragedies of Shakespeare; nevertheless, the difference is far greater than the likeness. In opera all is subordinated to the music, the dresses and the scenery; – the poetry is a mere vehicle for articulation, and as little pleasure is lost by ignorance of the Italian language, so little is gained by the knowledge of it. But in the Greek drama all was but as instruments and accessories to the poetry; and hence we should form a better notion of the choral music from the solemn hymns and psalms of austere church music than from any species of theatrical singing. A single flute or pipe was the ordinary accompaniment; and it is not to be supposed, that any display of musical power was allowed to obscure the distinct hearing of the words. On the contrary, the evident purpose was to render the words more audible, and to secure by the elevations and pauses greater facility of understanding the poetry. For the choral songs are, and ever must have been, the most difficult part of the tragedy; there occur in them the most involved verbal compounds, the newest expressions, the boldest images, the most recondite allusions. Is it credible that the poets would, one and all, have been thus prodigal of the stores of art and genius, if they had known that in the representation the whole must have been lost to the audience, – at a time too, when the means of after publication were so difficult and expensive, and the copies of their works so slowly and narrowly circulated?

The masks also must be considered – their vast variety and admirable workmanship. Of this we retain proof by the marble masks which represented them; but to this in the real mask we must add the thinness of the substance and the exquisite fitting on the head of the actor; so that not only were the very eyes painted with a single opening left for the pupil of the actor's eye, but in some instances even the iris itself was painted, when the colour was a known characteristic of the divine or heroic personage represented.

Finally, I will note down those fundamental characteristics which contradistinguish the ancient literature from the modern generally, but which more especially appear in prominence in the tragic drama. The ancient was allied to statuary, the modern refers to painting. In the first there is a predominance of rhythm and melody, in the second of harmony and counterpoint. The Greeks idolized the finite, and therefore were the masters of all grace, elegance, proportion, fancy, dignity, majesty – of whatever, in short, is capable of being definitely conveyed by defined forms or thoughts: the moderns revere the infinite, and affect the indefinite as a vehicle of the infinite; – hence their passions, their obscure hopes and fears, their wandering through the unknown, their grander moral feelings, their more august conception of man as man, their future rather than their past – in a word, their sublimity . . .

If the tragedies of Sophocles are in the strictest sense of the word tragedies, and the comedies of Aristophanes comedies, we must emancipate ourselves from a false association arising from misapplied names, and find a new word for the plays of Shakespeare. For they are, in the ancient sense, neither tragedies nor comedies, nor both in one, – but a different *genus*, diverse in kind, and not merely different in degree. They may be called romantic dramas, or dramatic romances.

A deviation from the simple forms and unities of the ancient stage is an essential principle, and, of course, an appropriate excellence, of the romantic drama. For these unities were to a great extent the natural form of that which in its elements was homogeneous, and the representation of which was addressed pre-eminently to the outward senses; – and though the fable, the language and the characters appealed to the reason rather than to the mere understanding, inasmuch as they supposed an ideal state rather than referred to an existing reality, – yet it was a reason which was obliged to accommodate itself to the senses, and so far became a sort of more elevated understanding. On the other hand, the romantic poetry – the Shakespearean drama – appealed to the imagination rather than to the senses, and to the reason as contemplating our inward nature, and the workings of the passions in their most retired recesses. But the reason, as reason, is independent of time and space; it has nothing to do with them: and hence the certainties of reason have been called eternal truths. As for example – the endless properties of the circle: what connection have they with this or that age, with this or that country? – The reason is aloof from time and space; the imagination is an arbitrary controller over both; – and if only the poet have such power of exciting our internal emotions as to make us present to the scene in imagination chiefly, he acquires the right and privilege of using time and space as they exist in imagination, and obedient only to the laws by which imagination itself acts. These laws it will be my object and aim to point out as the examples occur, which illustrate them. But here let me remark what can never be too often reflected on by all who would intelligently study the works either of the Athenian dramatists, or of Shakespeare, that the very essence of the former consists in the sternest separation of the diverse in kind and the disparate in the degree, whilst the latter delights in interlacing, by a rainbow-like transfusion of hues, the one with the other . . .

The true stage-illusion in this and in all other things consists – not in the mind's judging it to be a forest, but, in its remission of the judgment that it is not a forest. And this subject of stage-illusion is so important, and so many practical errors and false criticism may arise, and indeed have arisen, either from reasoning on it as actual delusion, (the strange notion, on which the French critics built up their theory, and on which the French poets justify the construction of their tragedies), or from denying it altogether, (which seems the end of Dr. Johnson's reasoning, and which, as extremes meet, would lead to the very same consequences, by excluding whatever would not be judged probable by us in our coolest state of feeling, with all our faculties in even balance), that these few remarks will, I hope, be pardoned, if they should serve either to explain or to illustrate the point. For not only are we never absolutely deluded – or any thing like it, but the attempt to cause the highest delusion possible to beings in their senses sitting in a theatre, is a gross fault, incident only to low minds, which, feeling that they cannot affect the heart or head permanently, endeavour to call forth the momentary affections. There ought never to be more pain than is compatible with co-existing pleasure, and to be amply repaid by thought.

Shakespeare found the infant stage demanding an intermixture of ludicrous character as imperiously as that of Greece did the chorus, and high language accordant. And there are many advantages in this; – a greater assimilation to nature, a greater scope of power, more truths, and more feelings; – the effects of contrast, as in Lear and the Fool; and especially this, that the true language of passion becomes sufficiently elevated by your having previously heard, in the same piece, the lighter conversation of men under no strong emotion. The very nakedness of the stage, too, was advantageous, – for the drama thence became something between recitation and a representation; and the absence or paucity of scenes allowed a freedom from the laws of unity of place and unity of time, the observance of which must either confine the drama to as few subjects as may be counted on the fingers, or involve gross improbabilities, far more striking than the violation would have caused. Thence, also, was precluded the danger of a false ideal, – of aiming at more than what is possible on the whole. What play of the ancients, with reference to their ideal, does not hold out more glaring absurdities than any in Shakespeare? On the Greek plan a man could more easily be a poet than a dramatist; upon our plan more easily a dramatist than a poet . . .

Let me now proceed to destroy, as far as may be in my power, the popular notion that he was a great dramatist by mere instinct, that he grew immortal in his own despite, and sank below men of second or third-rate power, when he attempted aught beside the drama – even as bees construct their cells and manufacture their honey to admirable perfection; but would in vain attempt to build a nest. Now this mode of reconciling a compelled sense of inferiority with a feeling of pride, began in a few pedants, who having read that Sophocles was the great model of tragedy, and Aristotle the infallible dictator of its rules, and finding that the Lear, Hamlet, Othello and other masterpieces were neither in imitation of Sophocles, nor in obedience to Aristotle, – and not having (with one or two exceptions) the courage to affirm, that the delight which their country received from generation to generation, in defiance of the alterations of circumstances and habits, was wholly groundless, – took upon them as a happy medium and refuge, to talk of Shakespeare as a sort of beautiful *lusus naturae*, a delightful monster, – wild, indeed, and without taste or judgment, but like the inspired idiots so much venerated in the East, uttering amid the strangest follies, the sublimest truths . . .

Are the plays of Shakespeare works of rude uncultivated genius, in which the splendour of the parts compensates, if aught can compensate, for the barbarous shapelessness and irregularity of the whole? – Or is the form equally admirable with the matter, and the judgment of the great poet, not less deserving our wonder than his genius? – Or, again, to repeat the question in other words: – Is Shakespeare a great dramatic poet on account only of those beauties and excellences which he possesses in common with the ancients, but with diminished claims to our love and honour to the full extent of his differences from them? – Or are these very differences additional proofs of poetic wisdom, at once results and symbols of living power as contrasted with lifeless mechanism – of free and rival originality as contradistinguished from servile imitation, or, more accurately, a blind copying of effects, instead of a true imitation, of the essential principles? – Imagine not that I am about to oppose genius to rules. No! the comparative value of these rules is the very cause to be tried. The spirit of poetry, like all other living powers, must of necessity circumscribe itself by rules, were it only to unite power with beauty. It must embody in order to reveal itself; but a living body is of necessity an organized one; and what is organization but the connection of parts in and for a whole, so that each part is at once ends and means? – This is no discovery of criticism; – it is a necessity of the human mind; and all nations have felt and obeyed it, in the invention of metre, and measured sounds, as the vehicle and *involucrum* [wrapping or cover] of poetry – itself a fellow-growth from the same life, – even as the bark is to the tree!

No work of true genius dares want its appropriate form, neither indeed is there any danger of this. As it must not, so genius cannot, be lawless; for it is even this that constitutes its genius – the power of acting creatively under laws of its own origination. How then comes it that not only single *Zoili* [critics], but whole nations have combined in unhesitating condemnation of our great dramatist, as a sort of African nature, rich in beautiful monsters – as a wild heath where islands of fertility look the greener from the surrounding waste, where the loveliest plants now shine out among the unsightly weeds, and now are choked by their parasitic growth, so intertwined that we cannot disentangle the weed without snapping the flower? – In this statement I have had no reference to the vulgar abuse of Voltaire, save as far as his charges are coincident with the decisions of Shakespeare's own commentators and (so they would tell you) almost idolatrous admirers. The true ground of the mistake lies in the confounding mechanical regularity with organic form. The form is mechanic, when on any given material we impress a pre-determined form, not necessarily arising out of the properties of the material; – as when to a mass of wet clay we give whatever shape we wish it to retain when hardened. The organic form, on the other hand, is innate; it shapes, as it develops, itself from within, and the fulness of its development is one and the same with the perfection of its outward form. Such as the life is, such is the form. Nature, the prime genial artist, inexhaustible in diverse powers, is equally inexhaustible in forms; – each exterior is the physiognomy of the being within, – its true image reflected and thrown out from the concave mirror; – and even such is the appropriate excellence of her chosen poet, of our own Shakespeare, – himself a nature humanized, a genial understanding directing self-consciously a power and an implicit wisdom deeper even than our consciousness.

William Hazlitt
'On Poetry in General' (1818)

Like Coleridge, Hazlitt recognizes Shakespeare's poetic power, and concludes that the emotional appeal of poetic drama is allied to the human love of excitement; thus in his Romantic approach Hazlitt stresses the dramatic force of Shakespearean tragedy.

One mode in which the dramatic exhibition of passion excites our sympathy without raising our disgust is, that in proportion as it sharpens the edge of calamity and disappointment, it strengthens the desire of good. It enhances our consciousness of the blessing, by making us sensible of the magnitude of the loss. The storm of passion lays bare and shows us the rich depths of the human soul: the whole of our existence, the sum total of our passions and pursuits, of that which we desire and that which we dread, is brought before us by contrast; the action and re-action are equal; the keenness of immediate suffering only gives us a more intense aspiration after, and a more intimate participation with the antagonist world of good; makes us drink deeper of the cup of human life; tugs at the heart strings; loosens the pressure about them; and calls the springs of thought and feeling into play with tenfold force.

Impassioned poetry is an emanation of the moral and intellectual part of our nature, as well as of the sensitive – of the desire to know, the will to act, and the power to feel; and ought to appeal to these different parts of our constitution, in order to be perfect. The domestic prose tragedy, which is thought to be the most natural, is in this sense the least so, because it appeals almost exclusively to one of these faculties, our sensibility. The tragedies of Moore and Lillo, for this reason, however affecting at the time, oppress and lie like a dead weight upon the mind, a load of misery which it is unable to throw off: the tragedy of Shakespeare, which is true poetry, stirs our inmost affections; abstracts evil from itself by combining it with all the forms of imagination, and with the deepest workings of the heart, and rouses the whole man within us.

The pleasure, however, derived from tragic poetry, is not any thing peculiar to it as poetry, as a fictitious and fanciful thing. It is not an anomaly of the imagination. It has its source and groundwork in the common love of strong excitement. As Mr Burke observes, people flock to see a tragedy; but if there were a public execution in the next street, the theatre would very soon be empty. It is not then the difference between fiction and reality that solves the difficulty. Children are satisfied with the stories of ghosts and witches in plain prose: nor do the hawkers of full, true, and particular accounts of murders and executions about the streets, find it necessary to have them turned into penny ballads, before they can dispose of these interesting and authentic documents. The grave politician drives a thriving trade of abuse and calumnies poured out against those whom he makes his enemies for no other end than that he may live by them. The popular preacher makes less frequent mention of heaven than of hell. Oaths and nicknames are only a more vulgar sort of poetry or rhetoric. We are as fond of indulging our violent passions as of reading a description of those of others. We are as prone to make a torment of our fears, as to luxuriate in our hopes of good. If it be asked, Why we do so? the best answer will be, Because we cannot help it. The sense of power is as strong a principle in the mind as the love of pleasure. Objects of terror and pity exercise the same despotic control over it as those of love or beauty. It is as natural to hate as to love, to despise as to admire, to express our hatred or contempt, as our love or admiration.

'On Shakespeare and Milton' (1818)

Hazlitt anticipates later critical trends in concentrating on Shakespeare's language, and he stresses its variety and richness. He places Shakespearean tragedy in its context, acknowledging Shakespeare's faults as well as the universality of his appeal.

Shakespeare's language and versification are like the rest of him. He has a magic power over words: they come winged at his bidding; and seem to know their places. They are struck out at a heat, on the spur of the occasion, and have all the truth and vividness which arise from an actual impression of the objects. His epithets and single phrases are like sparkles, thrown off from an imagination, fired by the whirling rapidity of its own motion. His language is hieroglyphical. It translates thoughts into visible images. It abounds in sudden transitions and elliptical expressions. This is the source of his mixed metaphors, which are only abbreviated forms of speech. These, however, give no pain from long custom. They have, in fact, become idioms in the language. They are the building, and not the scaffolding to thought. We take the meaning and effect of a well-known passage entire, and no more stop to scan and spell out the particular words and phrases, than the syllables of which they are composed. In trying to recollect any other author, one sometimes stumbles, in case of failure, on a word as good. In Shakespeare, any other word but the true one, is sure to be wrong. If any body, for instance, could not recollect the words of the following description,

> '- Light thickens,
> And the crow makes wing to the rooky wood,'

he would be greatly at a loss to substitute others for them equally expressive of the feeling. These remarks, however, are strictly applicable only to the impassioned parts of Shakespeare's language, which flowed from the warmth and originality of his imagination, and were his own. The language used for prose conversation and ordinary business is sometimes technical, and involved in the affectation of the time. Compare, for example, Othello's apology to the senate, relating 'his whole course of love,' with some of the preceding parts relating to his appointment, and the official dispatches from Cyprus. In this respect, 'the business of the state does him offence.' His versification is no less powerful, sweet, and varied. It has every occasional excellence, of sullen intricacy, crabbed and perplexed, or of the smoothest and loftiest expansion – from the ease and familiarity of measured conversation to the lyrical sounds

> '- Of ditties highly penned,
> Sung by a fair queen in a summer's bower,
> With ravishing division of her lute.'

It is the only blank verse in the language, except Milton's, that for itself is readable. It is not stately and uniformly swelling like his, but varied and broken by the inequalities of the ground it has to pass over in its uncertain course,

> 'And so by many winding nooks it strays,
> With willing sport to the wild ocean.'

It remains to speak of the faults of Shakespeare. They are not so many or so great as they have been represented; what there are, are chiefly owing to the following causes: – The universality of his genius was, perhaps, a disadvantage to his single works; the variety of his resources, sometimes diverting him from applying them to the most effectual purposes. He might be said to combine the powers of Aeschylus and Aristophanes, of Dante and Rabelais, in his own mind. If he had been only half what he was, he would perhaps have appeared greater. The natural ease and indifference of his temper made him sometimes less scrupulous than he might have been. He is relaxed and careless in critical places; he is in earnest throughout only in Timon, Macbeth, and Lear. Again, he had no models of acknowledged excellence constantly in view to stimulate his efforts, and by all that appears, no love of fame. He wrote for the 'great vulgar and the small,' in his time, not for posterity. If Queen Elizabeth and the maids of honour laughed heartily at his worst jokes, and the catcalls in the gallery were silent at his best passages, he went home satisfied, and slept the next night well. He did not trouble himself about Voltaire's criticisms. He was willing to take advantage of the ignorance of the age in many things; and if his plays pleased others, not to quarrel with them himself. His very facility of production would make him set less value on his own excellences, and not care to distinguish nicely between what he did well or ill. His blunders in chronology and geography do not amount to above half a dozen, and they are offences against chronology and geography, not against poetry. As to the unities, he was right in setting them at defiance. He was fonder of puns than became so great a man. His barbarisms were those of his age. His genius was his own. He had no objection to float down with the stream of common taste and opinion: he rose above it by his own buoyancy, and an impulse which he could not keep under, in spite of himself or others, and 'his delights did shew most dolphin-like.'

He had an equal genius for comedy and tragedy; and his tragedies are better than his comedies, because tragedy is better than comedy. His female characters, which have been found fault with as insipid, are the finest in the world. Lastly, Shakespeare was the least of a coxcomb of any one that ever lived, and much of a gentleman.

Thomas De Quincey
'A Summary Survey' (1838)

In this short article on Shakespeare for an Encyclopaedia De Quincey praises the female characters of the plays. As did Coleridge, De

Quincey compares the warmth of Shakespeare's portrayals with the cold exemplars of Greek tragedy. He realized the importance of the female characters in Shakespearean tragedy, but notably stressed the organic role of character within the dramatic context.

In the gravest sense it may be affirmed of Shakespeare that he is among the modern luxuries of life; that life, in fact, is a new thing, and one more to be coveted since Shakespeare has extended the domains of human consciousness, and pushed back its dark frontiers into regions not so much as dimly descried or even suspected before his time, far less illuminated (as now they are) by beauty and tropical luxuriance of life. For instance, – a single instance, indeed one which in itself is a world of new revelation, – the possible beauty of the female character had not been seen in a drama before Shakespeare called into perfect life the radiant shapes of Desdemona, of Imogen, of Hermione, of Perdita, of Ophelia, of Miranda, and many others. The Una of Spenser, earlier by ten to fifteen years than most of these, was an idealized portrait of female innocence and virgin purity, but too shadowy and unreal for a dramatic reality. And as to the Grecian classics, let not the reader imagine for an instant that any prototype in this field of Shakespearean power can be looked for there. The *Antigone* and the *Electra* of the tragic poets are the two leading female characters that classical antiquity offers to our respect, but assuredly not to our impassioned love, as disciplined and exalted in the school of Shakespeare. They challenge our admiration, severe, even stern, as impersonations of filial duty, cleaving to the steps of a desolate and afflicted old man; or of sisterly affection, maintaining the rights of a brother under circumstances of peril, of desertion, and consequently of perfect self-reliance. Iphigenia, again, though not dramatically coming before us in her own person, but according to the beautiful report of a spectator, presents us with a fine statuesque model of heroic fortitude, and of one whose young heart, even in the very agonies of her cruel immolation, refused to forget, by a single indecorous gesture, or so much as a moment's neglect of her own princely descent, that she herself was 'a lady in the land.' These are fine marble groups, but they are not the warm breathing realities of Shakespeare; there is 'no speculation' in their cold marble eyes; the breath of life is not in their nostrils; the fine pulses of womanly sensibilities are not throbbing in their bosoms. And besides this immeasurable difference between the cold moonly reflexes of life, as exhibited by the power of Grecian art, and the true sunny life of Shakespeare, it must be observed that the Antigones, etc., of the antique put forward but one single trait of character, like the aloe with its single blossom: this solitary figure is presented to us as an abstraction, and as an insulated quality; whereas in Shakespeare all is presented in the *concrete*; that is to say, not brought forward in relief, as by some effort of an anatomical artist; but embodied and embedded, so to speak, as by the force of a creative nature, in the complex system of a human life; a life in which all the elements move and play simultaneously, and with something more than mere simultaneity or co-existence, acting and re-acting each upon the other – nay, even acting by each other and through each other. In Shakespeare's characters is felt for ever a real *organic* life, where each is for the whole and in the whole, and where the whole is for each and in each. They only are real incarnations.

Edward Dowden
Shakspere: A Critical Study of his Mind and Art (1875)

Shakespeare's personal life and intellectual development is related to the canon of the works in Dowden's approach, and he identifies as a distinctive period the ferment of the great tragedies, to be followed by the supposed personal tranquility of the final romances. This approach was not without value, for instance in its attempt at synthesis and its recognition that Shakespeare was no superficial moralist, but its generalized sentimentality and assumptions about the creative personality were the least satisfactory legacy of Victorian criticism.

At first in the career of most artists a portion of their nature holds aloof from art, and is ready for application to other service. They have a poetical side, and a side which is prosaic. Gradually, as they advance towards maturity, faculty after faculty is brought into fruitful relation with the art-instinct, until at length the entire nature of the artist is fused in one, and his work becomes the expression of a complete personality. This period had now arrived for Shakespere. In the great tragedies passion and thought, humour and pathos, severity and tenderness, knowledge and guess, are all accepted as workers together with the imagination.

Tragedy as conceived by Shakspere is concerned with the ruin or the restoration of the soul, and of the life of men. In other words its subject is the struggle of good and evil in the world. . . .

There are certain problems which Shakspere at once pronounces insoluble. He does not, like Milton, propose to give any account of the origin of evil. He does not, like Dante, pursue the soul of man through circles of unending torture, or spheres made radiant by the eternal presence of God. Satan in Shakspere's poems does not come voyaging on gigantic vans across Chaos to find the earth. No great deliverer of mankind descends from the heavens. Here, upon the earth, evil *is* – such was Shakspere's declaration in the most emphatic accent. Iago actually exists. There is also in the earth a sacred passion of deliverance, a pure redeeming ardour. Cordelia exists. This Shakspere can tell for certain. But how Iago can be, and why Cordelia lies strangled across the breast of Lear – are these questions which you go on to ask? Something has been already said of the severity of Shakspere. It is a portion of his severity to decline all answers to such questions as these. Is Ignorance painful? Well, then, it is painful. Little solutions of your large difficulties can readily be obtained from priest or *philosophe*. Shakspere prefers to let you remain in the solemn presence of a mystery. He does not invite you into his little church or his little library brilliantly illuminated by philosophical or theological rushlights. You remain in the darkness. But you remain in the vital air. And the great night is overhead. . . .

This period during which Shakspere was engaged upon his great tragedies was not, as it has been sometimes represented, a period of depression and of gloom in Shakspere's spiritual progress. True, he was now sounding the depths of evil as he had never sounded them before. But his faith in goodness had never been so strong and sure. Hitherto it had not been thoroughly tested. In the over-strained loyalty of Valentine to his unworthy friend there is something fantastic and unreal. The graver friendship of Horatio and Hamlet is deeper and more genuine. There is gallantry in Portia's rescue of her husband's friend from death; but the devotion of Cordelia nourishes itself from springs of strength which lie farther down among the roots of things. Now, with every fresh discovery of crime Shakspere made discovery of virtue which cannot suffer defeat. The knowledge of evil and of good grow together. While Shakspere moved gaily upon the surface of life, it was the play of intellect that stirred within him the liveliest sense of pleasure. The bright speech and unsubduable mirth, not disjoined from common sense and goodness of heart of a Rosalind or a Beatrice, filled him with a sense of quickened existence. Now that he had come to comprehend more of the sorrow and more of the evil of the earth – treachery, ingratitude, cruelty, lust – Shakspere found perhaps less to delight him in mere brightness of intellect; he certainly gave his heart away with more fervour of loyalty to human goodness, to fortitude, purity of heart, self-surrender, self-mastery – to every noble expression of character. Such mellowing and enriching of Shakspere's nature could not have proceeded during a period in which his moral being was in confusion, and heaven and earth seemed to lie chaotically around him. Were his delight in man and woman, his faith and joy in human goodness, stained with sullenness and ignoble resentment, could he have discovered Horatio and Kent, Cordelia and Desdemona? No. If the sense of wrong sank deep into his soul, if life became harder and more grave, yet he surmounted all sense of personal wrong, and while life grew more severe, it grew more beautiful.

A. C. Bradley
Shakespearean Tragedy (1904)

The rationale of the approach to Shakespearean tragedy through character in the first part of Bradley's famous lectures is still worth serious consideration, despite the critical reaction against the excessive use of character analysis which followed. It is notable, for instance, that Bradley insists on the primacy of Shakespeare as a dramatist, that he distinguishes between plot and tragic action, that mental disturbance and the supernatural are put in dramatic perspective. For Bradley the mental struggle of the tragic hero reflecting the external struggle of the action, was the key approach to the central conflict of Shakespearean tragedy. The emphasis may need to be moderated, but Bradley's critical approach should not be dismissed completely.

The 'story' or 'action' of a Shakespearean tragedy does not consist, of course, solely of human actions or deeds; but the deeds are the predominant factor. And these deeds are, for the most part, actions in the full sense of the word; not things done ' 'tween asleep and wake', but acts or omissions thoroughly expressive of the doer, – character-istic deeds. The centre of the tragedy, therefore, may be said with equal truth to lie in action issuing from character, or in character issuing in action.

Shakespeare's main interest lay here. To say that it lay in *mere* character, or was a psychological interest, would be a great mistake, for he was dramatic to the tips of his fingers. It is possible to find places where he has given a certain indulgence to his love of poetry, and even to his turn for general reflections; but it would be very difficult, and in his later tragedies perhaps impossible, to detect passages where he has allowed such freedom to the interest in character apart from action. But for the opposite extreme, for the abstraction of mere 'plot' (which is a very different thing from the tragic 'action'), for the kind of interest which predominates in a novel like *The Woman in White*, it is clear that he cared even less. I do not mean that this interest is absent from his dramas; but it is subordinate to others, and is so interwoven with them that we are rarely conscious of it apart, and rarely feel in any great strength the half-intellectual, half-nervous excitement of following an ingenious complication. What we do feel strongly, as a tragedy advances to its close, is that the calamities and catastrophe follow inevitably from the deeds of men, and that the main source of the deeds is character. The dictum that, with Shakespeare, 'character is destiny' is no doubt an exaggeration, and one that may mislead (for many of his tragic personages, if they had not met with peculiar circumstances, would have escaped a tragic end, and might even have lived fairly untroubled lives); but it is the exaggeration of a vital truth.

This truth, with some of its qualifications, will appear more clearly if we now go on to ask what elements are to be found in the 'story' or 'action', occasionally or frequently, beside the characteristic deeds, and the sufferings and circumstances, of the persons. I will refer to three of these additional factors.

(*a*) Shakespeare, occasionally and for reasons which need not be discussed here, represents abnormal conditions of mind; insanity, for example, somnambulism, hallucinations. And deeds issuing from these are certainly not what we called deeds in the fullest sense, deeds expressive of character. No; but these abnormal conditions are never introduced as the origin of deeds of any dramatic moment. Lady Macbeth's sleep-walking has no influence whatever on the events that follow it. Macbeth did not murder Duncan because he saw a dagger in the air: he saw the dagger because he was about to murder Duncan. Lear's insanity is not the cause of a tragic conflict any more than

Ophelia's; it is, like Ophelia's, the result of a conflict; and in both cases the effect is mainly pathetic. If Lear were really mad when he divided his kingdom, if Hamlet were really mad at any time in the story, they would cease to be tragic characters.

(*b*) Shakespeare also introduces the supernatural into some of his tragedies; he introduces ghosts, and witches who have supernatural knowledge. This supernatural element certainly cannot in most cases, if in any, be explained away as an illusion in the mind of one of the characters. And further, it does contribute to the action, and is in more than one instance an indispensable part of it: so that to describe human character, with circumstances, as always the *sole* motive force in this action would be a serious error. But the supernatural is always placed in the closest relation with character. It gives a confirmation and a distinct form to inward movements already present and exerting influence; to the sense of failure in Brutus, to the stifled workings of conscience in Richard, to the half-formed thought or the horrified memory of guilt in Macbeth, to suspicion in Hamlet. Moreover, its influence is never of a compulsive kind. It forms no more than an element, however important, in the problem which the hero has to face; and we are never allowed to feel that it has removed his capacity or responsibility for dealing with this problem. So far indeed are we from feeling this, that many readers run to the opposite extreme, and openly or privately regard the supernatural as having nothing to do with the real interest of the play.

(*c*) Shakespeare, lastly, in most of his tragedies allows to 'chance' or 'accident' an appreciable influence at some point in the action. Chance or accident here will be found, I think, to mean any occurrence (not supernatural, of course) which enters the dramatic sequence neither from the agency of a character, nor from the obvious surrounding circumstances. It may be called an accident, in this sense, that Romeo never got the Friar's message about the potion, and that Juliet did not awake from her long sleep a minute sooner; an accident that Edgar arrived at the prison just too late to save Cordelia's life; an accident that Desdemona dropped her handkerchief at the most fatal of moments; an accident that the pirate ship attacked Hamlet's ship, so that he was able to return forthwith to Denmark. Now this operation of accident is a fact, and a prominent fact, of human life. To exclude it *wholly* from tragedy, therefore, would be, we may say, to fail truth. And, besides, it is not merely a fact. That men may start a course of events but can neither calculate nor control it, is a *tragic* fact. The dramatist may use accident so as to make us feel this; and there are also other dramatic uses to which it may be put. Shakespeare accordingly admits it. On the other hand, any *large* admission of chance into the tragic sequence would certainly weaken, and might destroy, the sense of the causal connection of character, deed, and catastrophe. And Shakespeare really uses it very sparingly. We seldom find ourselves exclaiming, 'What an unlucky accident!' I believe most readers would have to search painfully for instances. It is, further, frequently easy to see the dramatic intention of an accident; and some things which look like accidents have really a connection with character, and are therefore not in the full sense accidents. Finally, I believe it will be found that almost all the prominent accidents occur when the action is well advanced and the impression of the causal sequence is too firmly fixed to be impaired.

Thus it appears that these three elements in the 'action' are subordinate, while the dominant factor consists in deeds which issue from character. So that, by way of summary, we may now alter our first statement, 'A tragedy is a story of exceptional calamity leading to the death of a man in high estate,' and we may say instead (what in its turn is one-sided, though less so), that the story is one of human actions producing exceptional calamity and ending in the death of such a man.

Before we leave the 'action,' however, there is another question that may usefully be asked. Can we define this 'action' further by describing it as a conflict?

The frequent use of this idea in discussion on tragedy is ultimately due, I suppose, to the influence of Hegel's theory on the subject, certainly the most important theory since Aristotle's. But Hegel's view of the tragic conflict is not only unfamiliar to English readers and difficult to expound shortly, but it had its origin in reflections on Greek tragedy and, as Hegel was well aware, applies only imperfectly to the works of Shakespeare. I shall, therefore, confine myself to the idea of conflict in its more general form. In this form it is obviously suitable to Shakespearean tragedy; but it is vague, and I will try to make it more precise by putting the question. Who are the combatants in this conflict?

Not seldom the conflict may quite naturally be conceived as lying between two persons, of whom the hero is one; or, more fully, as lying between two parties or groups, in one of which the hero is the leading figure. Or if we prefer to speak (as we may quite well do if we know what we are about) of the passions, tendencies, ideas, principles, forces, which animate these passions or groups, we may say that two such passions or ideas, regarded as animating two persons or groups, are the combatants. The love of Romeo and Juliet is in conflict with the hatred of their houses, represented by various other characters. The cause of Brutus and Cassius struggles with that of Julius, Octavius and Antony. In *Richard II* the King stands on one side, Bolingbroke and his party on the other. In *Macbeth* the hero and heroine are opposed to the representatives of Duncan. In all these cases the great majority of the *dramatis personae* fall without difficulty into antagonistic groups, and the conflict between these groups ends with the defeat of the hero.

Yet one cannot help feeling that in at least one of these cases, *Macbeth*, there is something a little external in this way of looking at the action. And when we come to some other plays this feeling increases. No doubt most of the characters in *Hamlet*, *King Lear*, *Othello*, or *Antony and Cleopatra* can be arranged in opposed groups; and no doubt there is conflict; and yet it seems misleading to describe this conflict as one *between these groups*. It cannot be simply this. For though Hamlet and the King are mortal foes, yet that which engrosses our interest and dwells in our memory at least as much as the conflict between them, is the conflict *within* one of them. And so it is, though not in the same degree, with *Antony and Cleopatra* and even in *Othello*; and, in fact, in a certain measure, it is so with nearly all the tragedies. There is an outward conflict of persons or groups, there is also a conflict of forces in the hero's soul; and even in *Julius Caesar* and *Macbeth* the interest of the former can hardly be said to exceed that of the latter.

The truth is, that the type of tragedy in which the hero opposes to a hostile force an undivided soul, is not the Shakespearean type. The souls of those who contend with the hero may be thus undivided; they generally are; but, as a rule, the hero, though he pursues his fated way, is, at least at some point in the action, and sometimes at many, torn by an inward struggle; and it is frequently at such points that Shakespeare shows his most extraordinary power. If further we compare the earlier tragedies with the later, we find that it is in the latter, the maturest works, that this inward struggle is most emphasized. In the last of them, *Coriolanus*, its interest completely eclipses towards the close of the play that of the outward conflict. *Romeo and Juliet*, *Richard III*, *Richard II*, where the hero contends with an outward force, but comparatively little with himself, are all early plays.

If we are to include the outer and the inner struggle in a conception more definite than that of conflict in general we must employ some such phrase as 'spiritual force.' This will mean whatever forces act in the human spirit, whether good or evil, whether personal passion or impersonal principle; doubts, desires, scruples, ideas – whatever can animate, shake, possess, and drive a man's soul. In a Shakespearean tragedy some such forces are shown in conflict. They are shown acting in men and generating strife between them. They are also shown, less universally, but quite as characteristically, generating disturbance and even conflict in the soul of the hero. Treasonous ambition in Macbeth collides with loyalty and patriotism in Macduff and Malcolm: here is the outward conflict. But these powers or principles equally collide in the soul of Macbeth himself: here is the inner. And neither by itself could make the tragedy.

We shall see later the importance of this idea. Here we need only observe that the notion of tragedy as a conflict emphasizes the fact that action is the centre of the story, while the concentration of interest, in the greater plays, on the inward struggle emphasizes the fact that this action is essentially the expression of character.

Walter Raleigh
Shakespeare (1907)

This rejection of a simplistic moral interpretation of Shakespearean tragedy is characteristic of much twentieth-century criticism. Raleigh's approach to character changes Bradley's emphasis and reflects the tendency to identify sympathetically with the tragic hero. The question of individual choice in tragedy reflects the classical concept, dramatically voiced in Anouilh's 1943 version of the Antigone: *'Tragedy is restful, and the reason is that hope, that foul deceitful thing, has no part in it. There isn't any hope. You're trapped.'*

There is no moral lesson to be read, except accidentally, in any of Shakespeare's tragedies. They deal with greater things than man; with powers and passions, elemental forces, and dark abysses of suffering; with the central fire, which breaks through the thin crust of civilisation, and makes a splendour in the sky above the blackness of ruined homes. Because he is a poet, and has a true imagination, Shakespeare knows how precarious is man's tenure of the soil, how deceitful are his quiet orderly habits and his prosaic speech. At any moment, by the operation of chance, or fate, these things may be broken up, and the world given over once more to the forces that struggle in chaos.

It is not true to say that in these tragedies character is destiny. Othello is not a jealous man; he is a man carried off his feet, wave-drenched and blinded by the passion of love. Macbeth is not a murderous politician; he is a man possessed. Lear no doubt has faults; he is irritable and exacting, and the price that he pays for these weaknesses in old age is that they let loose hell. Hamlet is sensitive, thoughtful, generous, impulsive, – 'a pure, noble, and most moral nature' – yet he does not escape the extreme penalty, and at the bar of a false criticism he too is made guilty of the catastrophe. But Shakespeare, who watched his heroes, awestruck, as he saw them being drawn into the gulf, passed no such judgment on them. In his view of it, what they suffer is out of all proportion to what they do and are. They are presented with a choice, and the essence of the tragedy is that choice is impossible. Coriolanus has to choose between the pride of his country and the closest of human affections. Antony stands poised between love and empire. Macbeth commits a foul crime; but Shakespeare's tragic stress is laid on the hopelessness of the dilemma that follows, and his great pity for mortality makes the crime a lesser thing. Hamlet fluctuates between the thought which leads nowhither and the action which is narrow and profoundly unsatisfying. Brutus, like Coriolanus, has to choose between his highest political hopes and the private ties of humanity. Lear's misdoing is forgotten in the doom that falls upon him; after his fit of jealous anger he awakens to find that he has no further choice, and is driven into the wilderness, a scapegoat for mankind. Othello – but the story of Othello exemplifies a further reach of Shakespeare's fearful irony – Othello, like Hamlet, suffers for his very virtue, and the noblest qualities of his mind are made the instruments of his crucifixion.

Levin Ludwig Schücking
Character Problems in Shakespeare's Plays (1922)

In his examination of Elizabethan stage techniques such as the soliloquy Shücking opposes the emphasis on psychological realism in approaches to character. His insistence that Shakespearean drama was generally more primitive than hitherto supposed argues for a new concept of a tragic figure such as Hamlet.

In drawing attention to the simplicity of the soliloquizing actor who allows his audience to look behind his mask we have taken only a partial, though very characteristic, aspect of this technical device. It is not true that the Shakespearean drama shows the traces of a more primitive time only in this one respect, while closely resembling the modern drama in all others. The primitiveness and a certain childishness manifested in the traits with which we have so far become acquainted is apparent, less distinctly, perhaps, but recognizable on closer scrutiny, in the whole mechanism of the Shakespearean drama. All the details of the technique are more harmless, simple, unsophisticated, than we are inclined to imagine. The monologue is not the only and not the most important among the naïve devices used for enlightening the audience. In the course of the play – that is, in the actual dialogue – the characters on the stage supply the audience with the most important information about themselves and reveal the innermost secrets of their nature. In a number of cases, it is true, most people will not regard this practice as a clumsy technical device, but rather look upon it as a tendency of the author to endow his figures with an inclination toward introspection, most probably without any conscious intention of throwing light upon the mental features of his personages for the spectators' benefit. Where this inclination is unobtrusive and incorporated in other similar traits, as, for example, the habit of self-reproach, it will at once escape the suspicion of being merely a primitive and intentional device. Nevertheless, these instances also are worthy of note. A case in point is to be found in *Hamlet*. The great majority of serious critics are agreed on the necessity of conceiving Hamlet not as a man of action, but essentially as a man of reflection. This reflection, however, is not only directed upon the world but also upon himself. The utterances of Hamlet in this latter respect are usually regarded as chiefly characterizing the subjective state of his soul. Indeed, who would take the railing and self-accusations, the insults with which he tries to spur himself to action, the doubts of himself, for Gospel truth? But while taking this view, we must not overlook that in this character we can discern Shakespeare's tendency to make his figures explain themselves in a manner which must be taken very seriously and which far transcends mere self-accusation and doubt.

Elmer Edgar Stoll
Art and Artifice in Shakespeare (1933)

A return from the primacy of character to the Aristotelian primacy of plot in the approach to tragedy is urged by Stoll, and he stresses the importance of the overall dramatic conflict. In this realistic approach he insists that drama is an illusion, and its characters should not be assessed as real people. The psychological effect on the audience of Shakespeare's dramatic poetry is more important than the psychological analysis of the characters created by his art and artifice.

The core of tragedy (and of comedy, too, for that matter) is situation; and a situation is a character in contrast, and perhaps also in conflict, with other characters or with circumstances. We have ordinarily been taught that with the author character comes first and foremost, not only in importance but in point of time, and (cause of no little confusion) that the action is only its issue. But there is no drama until the character is conceived in a complication; and in the dramatist's mind it is so conceived at the outset. This is when the whole is invented, as nowadays it is supposed to be: when, as with the ancients and the Elizabethans, an old story was used anew, then, obviously, the plot came foremost in time and the characters were invented to fit it. And not only in those days, but in any when drama has flourished, plot – not intrigue, of course, or external activity, but situation, which is its centre of energy – has been first in importance too. Even in this era of anarchy and chaos a drama in which the characters are presented *not* in a complication, is really none. Aristotle, who by literary and psychological critics has, regretfully, been taken to task for saying it, is justified by the facts: 'We maintain, therefore, that the first essential, the life and soul, so to speak, of Tragedy is the Plot; and that the characters come second . . . We maintain that Tragedy is primarily an imitation of action, and that it is mainly for the sake of the action that it imitates the personal agents.' And not really out of harmony with this is the subsequent precept, that 'whenever such-and-such a personage says or does such-and-such a thing, it shall be the probable or necessary outcome of his character.'

Unlike many critics today, the Stagirite [Aristotle] did not so much explore his own opinions and sensibilities as much as examine the practice of dramatists, who, then as now, were so eager for a good situation that, wherever found, they seized upon it, whether new or old. And the situation they have deemed the best is that in which the contrast or conflict is sharpest and most striking, the probability or psychological reasonableness of it being a secondary consideration. Indeed, in the greatest tragedies (and comedies and epics too) the situation has been fundamentally improbable, unreasonable. What are the greatest stories in the world? Those of Orestes, Oedipus, Achilles, and Odysseus; of Iphigeneia, Dido, Phaedra, Medea, and Herod and Mariamne; of Tristram and Isolt, Siegfried and Brunnhilde; of the Cid, Faustus, and Don Juan; of Lear, Othello, Macbeth, and Hamlet: all of them embodying situations improbable to an extreme degree. Their improbability is the price of their effectiveness: such fine and fruitful situations life itself does not afford. The sharper conflict provokes the bigger passion; the more striking contrast produces the bigger effect: and to genius the improbability is only a challenge . . .

Drama, therefore, if we are to judge of it from the foregoing, is no 'document'. (Not a social document, of course – that question has not here arisen – but not even a 'human' one.) Most of the misinterpretation of it, whether that of Shakespeare or of Aeschylus, has been more or less due to our taking it to be such. Whether as story or as character, it is, as Mr. Bridges says of Shakespeare's alone, 'not nature in the sense of being susceptible of the same analysis as that by which the assumptions of science would investigate nature'; and the tendency so to conceive of it is really the same spirit of literalism that prompted the sixteenth and seventeenth-century critics to establish the canon of the unities – the consideration that they afford, not (as they do) a more compact and effective structure, but a greater *vraisemblance*. The human figures certainly are not, as a recent writer has declared them to be, 'copied with little alteration from the population of the world'; and thank Heaven that they are not. Still less are they examples or illustrations of our psychology. But they are not always even perfect copies of the inner vision, that 'higher reality' which, as Goethe observes, great art represents. They are a compromise, an accommodation, a simplification, to suit the structure and particular conceptions of the whole. 'The spirit of man cannot be satisfied but with truth, or at least verisimility,' says Dryden, echoing Aristotle; but only verisimility is what art, drama, and more especially, among great drama, that of Shakespeare, bestow. It is not reality, or even perfect consistency, but an illusion, and, above all, an illusion whereby the spirit of man shall be moved. The greatest of dramatists is careful, not so much for the single character, as for the drama; indeed, he observes not so much the probabilities of the action, or the psychology of the character, as the psychology of the audience, for whom both the action and character are framed. Writing hastily, but impetuously, to be played, not read, he seizes upon almost every means of imitation and opportunity for excitement which this large liberty affords. For everything he would give us, not only (in effect) life as we know it, but (and far more) drama as we would have it be; yet remembers, no man so constantly, that the attention of his audience – the liberty of his art – has limits. Like all dramatists, he must have a situation; like all the greater dramatists, an intense one. He would, as would Dryden, 'work up the pity to a greater height.' Therefore, like them, he has, necessarily, had to start with premises or postulates, and provoke intrusions, human or superhuman, whereby the hero, still keeping our sympathy, can be put in a plight. And just because of the largeness of the undertaking – the whole story and an old one, many characters and situations, and times and places, not a few, and all the form and pressure, sound and colour, of existence – he has necessarily had – for consistency of illusion, swiftness of move-ment, and intensity of effect – to contrive more audaciously and variously, and (in turn) to make such amends or adjustments as he could, sometimes even by artifices which are scarcely art. He evades and hedges, he manœuvres and manipulates, he suppresses or obscures. But his most noble and effectual amends is positive – his poetry. The premise sets him free for it – *praecipitandus est liber spiritus* – and he walks not soberly afoot, like your philosopher, but flies. And Shakespeare is the greatest of the dramatists because the illusion he offers is the widest and highest, the emotion he arouses the most irresistible and overwhelming.

By poetry, an imaginative conquest, he works the wonder – by rhythm and recurrence, acceleration and retardation, swelling and subsidence, and this in the structure, the rhetoric, or the metre; also (for obviously drama is not music) by the seizing and ordering of such thoughts and sentiments, such words and images, as belong together, though never together in this world before; and (above all) in the characters, by both the one process and the other – and who knows by what other besides? – as a vitalizing, differentiating power. His imitation is creation; what with us is dull and solid fact, assumes, still recognizable, the potency and liberty of fiction. So it is, in some measure, with the Greeks as well, and with Racine and Ibsen, who one and all are poets, yet not in such a signal and pre-eminent measure, not to such dramatic – both airy and substantial – effect. They have less amends to make, but less resources wherewith to make them.

Shakespeare's characters, more unmistakably than anyone else's, are, from the outset, given voices, accents, of their own – and not individual only, but beautiful – a fact which inveigles us, throughout the play, and even (witness the critics) afterwards, into accepting, not them only, but also the incredible things that they not infrequently do. They speak – like human beings, though none we know or hear of – *therefore* they are; and then, if for nothing else, their story is – 'for the moment' – credible.

G. Wilson Knight
The Wheel of Fire (1930)

The extremes of psychological realism in the approach to character are castigated by Wilson Knight, who also finds the reaction of the 'realistic' critics with their theatrical emphasis unsatisfactory. He criticizes these approaches to Shakespearean tragedy as too superficial and pursues an imaginative critical path which seeks to penetrate the inner theme at the core of each play.

And finally as to 'character'. In the following essays the term is refused, since it is so constantly entwined with a false and unduly ethical criticism. So often we hear that 'in *Timon of Athens* it was Shakespeare's intention to show how a generous but weak character may come to ruin through an unwise use of his wealth'; that 'Shakespeare wished in *Macbeth* to show how crime inevitably brings retribution'; that, 'in *Antony and Cleopatra* Shakespeare has given us a lesson concerning the dangers of an uncontrolled passion'. These are purely imaginary examples, coloured for my purpose, to indicate the type of ethical criticism to which I refer. It continually brings in the intention-concept, which our moral-philosophy, rightly or wrongly, involves. Hence, too, the constant and fruitless search for 'motives' sufficient to account for Macbeth's and Iago's actions: since the moral critic feels he cannot blame a 'character' until he understands his 'intentions', and without the opportunity of praising and blaming he is dumb. It is not, clearly, possible to avoid ethical considerations; nor is it desirable. Where one person within the drama is immediately apparent as morally good and another as bad, we will note the difference: but we should follow our dramatic intuitions. A person in the drama may act in such a way that we are in no sense antagonized but are aware of beauty and supreme interest only; yet the analogy to that same action may well be intolerable to us in actual life. When such a divergence occurs the commentator must be true to his artistic, not his normal, ethic. Large quantities of Shakespeare criticism have wrecked themselves on the teeth of this dualism. In so far as moral values enter into our appreciation of the poetic work, they will tend to be instinctive to us: Shakespeare here, as in his other symbols, speaks our own language. I mean, it is as natural to us to like Cordelia better than Goneril with a liking which may be said to depend partly on moral values as it is for us to recognize the power of Shakespeare's tempest-symbol as suggesting human tragedy, or his use of jewel-metaphors to embody the costly riches of love. In ages hence, when perhaps tempests are controlled by science and communism has replaced wealth, then the point of Shakespeare's symbolism may need explanation; and then it may, from a new ethical viewpoint, be necessary to analyse at length the moral values implicit in the Cordelia and Edmund conceptions. But in these matters Shakespeare speaks almost the same language as we, and ethical terms, though they most frequently occur in interpretation, must only be allowed in so far as they are used in absolute obedience to the dramatic and aesthetic significance: in which case they cease to be ethical in the usual sense.

This false criticism is implied by the very use of the word 'character'. It is impossible to use the term without any tinge of morality which blurs vision. The term, which in ordinary speech often denotes the degree of moral control exercised by the individual over his instinctive passions, is altogether unsuited to those persons of poetic drama whose life consists largely of passion unveiled. *Macbeth* and *King Lear* are created in a soul-dimension of primal feeling, of which in real life we may be only partly conscious or may be urged to control by a sense of right and wrong. In fact, it may well seem that the more we tend away from the passionate and curbless life of poetic drama, the stronger we shall be as 'characters'. And yet, in reading *Macbeth* or *King Lear* we are aware of strength, not weakness. We are not aware of failure: rather we 'let determined things to destiny hold unbewailed their way.' We must observe, then, this paradox: the strong protagonist of poetic drama would probably appear a weakling if he were a real man; and, indeed, the critic who notes primarily Macbeth's weakness is criticizing him as a man rather than a dramatic person. Ethics are essentially critical when applied to life; but if they hold any place at all in art, they will need to be modified into a new artistic ethic which obeys the peculiar nature of art as surely as a sound morality is based on the nature of man. From a true interpretation centred on the imaginative qualities of Shakespeare, certain facts will certainly emerge which bear relevance to human life, to human morals: but interpretation must come first. And interpretation must be metaphysical rather than ethical. We shall gain nothing by applying to the delicate symbols of the poet's imagination the rough machinery of an ethical philosophy created to control the turbulences of actual life. Thus when a critic adopts the ethical attitude, we shall generally find that he is unconsciously lifting the object of his attention from his setting and regarding him as actually alive. By noting 'faults' in Timon's 'character' we are in effect saying that he would not be a success in real life: which is beside the point, since he, and Macbeth, and Lear, are evidently dramatic successes. Now, whereas the moral attitude to life is positive and dynamic and tells us what we ought to do, that attitude applied to literature is invariably negative and destructive. It is continually thrusting on our attention a number of 'failures', 'mistakes', and 'follies' in connexion with those dramatic persons from whom we have consistently derived delight and a sense of exultation. Even when terms of negation, such as 'evil', necessarily appear – as with *Hamlet* and *Macbeth* – we should so employ them that the essence they express is felt to be something powerful, autonomous, and grand. Our reaction to great literature is a positive and dynamic experience. Crudely, sometimes ineffectually, interpretation will attempt to translate that experience in a spirit also positive and dynamic.

To do this we should regard each play as a visionary whole, close-knit in personification, atmospheric suggestion, and direct poetic-symbolism: three modes of transmission, equal in their importance. Too often the first of these alone receives attention: whereas, in truth, we should not be content even with all three, however clearly we have them in our minds, unless we can work back through them to the original vision they express. Each incident, each turn of thought, each suggestive symbol throughout *Macbeth* or *King Lear* radiates inwards from the play's circumference to the burning central core without knowledge of which we shall miss their relevance and necessity: they relate primarily, not directly to each other, nor to the normal appearances of human life, but to this central reality alone. The persons of Shakespeare have been analysed carefully in point of psychological realism, yet in giving so detailed and prolix a care to any one element of the poet's expression, the commentator, starting indeed from a point on the circumference, instead of working into the heart of the play, pursues a tangential course, riding, as it were, on his own life-experiences farther and farther from his proper goal. Such is the criticism that finds fault with the Duke's decisions at the close of *Measure for Measure*: if we are to understand the persons of Shakespeare we should consider always what they do rather than what they might have done. Each person, event, scene, is integral to the poetic statement: the removing, or blurring, of a single stone in the mosaic will clearly lessen our chance of visualizing the whole design.

Too often the commentator discusses Shakespeare's work without the requisite emotional sympathy and agility of intellect. Then the process of false criticism sets in: whatever elements lend themselves most readily to analysis on the analogy of actual life, these he selects, roots out, distorting their natural growth; he then praises or blames according to their measure of correspondence with his own life-experiences, and, creating the plaster figures of 'character', searches everywhere for 'causes' on the analogy of human affairs, noting that Iago has no sufficient reason for his villainy, executing some strange transference such as the statement that Lady Macbeth would have done this or that in Cordelia's position; observing that there appears to have been dull weather on the occasion of Duncan's murder. But what he will not do is recapture for analysis his own original experience, concerned, as it was, purely with a dramatic and artistic reality: with Iago the person of motiveless and instinctive villainy, with Cordelia known only with reference to the *Lear* universe, with the vivid extravagant symbolism of abnormal phenomena in beast and element and the sun's eclipse which accompanies the unnatural act of murder. These, the true, the poetic, realities, the commentator too often passes over. He does not look straight at the work he would interpret, is not true to his own imaginative reaction. My complaint is, not that such a commentator cannot appreciate the imaginative nature of Shakespeare – that would be absurd and unjustifiable – but that he falsifies his own experience when he begins to criticize. Part of the play – and that the less important element of the story – he tears out ruthlessly for detailed analysis on the analogy of human life: with a word or two about 'the magic of the poetry' or 'the breath of genius' he dismisses the rest. Hence the rich gems of Shakespeare's poetic symbolism have been left untouched and unwanted, whilst Hamlet was being treated in Harley Street. Hence arises the criticism discovering faults in Shakespeare. But when a right interpretation is offered it will generally be seen that both the fault and the criticism which discovered it are without meaning. The older critics drove psychological analysis to unnecessary lengths: the new school of 'realistic' criticism, in finding faults and explaining them with regard to Shakespeare's purely practical and financial 'intentions', is thus in reality following the wrong vision of its predecessors. Both together trace the progress of my imaginary critic, who, thinking to have found an extreme degree of realism in one place, ends by complaining that he finds too little in another. Neither touch the heart of the Shakespearean play.

Nor will a sound knowledge of the stage and the especial theatrical technique of Shakespeare's work render up its imaginative secret. True, the plays were written as plays, and meant to be acted. But that tells us nothing relevant to our purpose. It explains why certain things cannot be found in Shakespeare: it does not explain why the finest things, the fascination of *Hamlet*, the rich music of *Othello*, the gripping evil of *Macbeth*, the pathos of *King Lear*, and the gigantic architecture of *Timon of Athens* came to birth. Shakespeare wrote in terms of drama, as he wrote in English. In the grammar of dramatic structure he expresses his vision: without that, or some other, structure he could not have expressed himself. But the dramatic nature of a play's origin cannot be adduced to disprove a quality implicit in the work itself. True, when there are any faults to be explained, this particular pursuit and aim of Shakespeare's poetry may well be noted to account for their presence. Interpretation, however, tends to resolve all but minor difficulties in connexion with the greater plays: therefore it is not necessary in the following essays to remember, or comment on, the dramatic structure of their expression, though from another point of view such comment and analysis may well be interesting. It illuminates one facet of their surface: but a true philosophic and imaginative interpretation will aim at cutting below the surface to reveal that burning core of mental or spiritual reality from which each play derives its nature and meaning.

Caroline Spurgeon
Shakespeare's Imagery and What it Tells Us (1935)

The approach to Shakespearean tragedy through language, and particularly the study of the significance of its iterative imagery, echoes Wilson Knight's emphasis on poetic theme rather than character. Caroline Spurgeon's pioneering work on imagery led her to see it as playing a significant part in arousing the tragic emotions of pity, fear, and horror; thus through the language of the poetry, with its subtle play upon the imagination, Shakespeare conveys the dramatic intensity of tragedy.

It is a curious thing that the part played by recurrent images in raising, developing, sustaining and repeating emotion in the tragedies has not, so far as I know, ever yet been noticed. It is a part somewhat analogous to the action of a recurrent theme or 'motif' in a musical fugue or sonata, or in one of Wagner's operas.

Perhaps, however, a more exact analogy to the function of Shakespeare's images in the tragedies is the unique work of another great artist, of the peculiar quality of which they constantly remind one, that is, Blake's illustrations of his prophetic books. These are not, for the most part, illustrations in the ordinary sense of the term, the translation by the artist of some incident in the narrative into a visual picture; they are rather a running accompaniment to the words in another medium, sometimes symbolically emphasising or interpreting certain aspects of the thought, sometimes supplying frankly only decoration or atmosphere, sometimes grotesque or even repellent, vivid, strange, arresting, sometimes drawn with an almost unearthly beauty of form and colour. Thus, as the leaping tongues of flame which illuminate the pages of *The Marriage of Heaven and Hell* show the visual form which Blake's thought evoked in his mind, and symbolise for us the purity, the beauty and the two-edged quality of life and danger in his words, so the recurrent images in *Macbeth* or *Hamlet* reveal the dominant picture or sensation – and for Shakespeare the two are identical – in terms of which he sees and feels the main problem or theme of the play, thus giving us an unerring clue to the way he looked at it, as well as a direct glimpse into the working of his mind and imagination.

In *Romeo and Juliet* the beauty and ardour of young love are seen by Shakespeare as the irradiating glory of sunlight and starlight in a dark world. The dominating image is *light*, every form and manifestation of it: the sun, moon, stars, fire, lightning, the flash of gunpowder, and the reflected light of beauty and of love; while by contrast we have night, darkness, clouds, rain, mist and smoke . . .

In *Hamlet*, naturally, we find ourselves in an entirely different atmosphere. If we look closely we see this is partly due to the number of images of sickness, disease or blemish of the body, in the play, and we discover that the idea of an ulcer or tumour, as descriptive of the unwholesome condition of Denmark morally, is, on the whole, the dominating one. . . .

To Shakespeare's pictorial imagination, therefore, the problem in *Hamlet* is not predominately that of will and reason, of a mind too philosophic or a nature temperamentally unfitted to act quickly; he sees it pictorially *not as the problem of an individual at all,* but as something greater and even more mysterious, as a *condition* for which the individual himself is apparently not responsible, any more than the sick man is to blame for the infection which strikes and devours him, but which, nevertheless, in its course and development, impartially and relentlessly, annihilates him and others, innocent and guilty alike. That is the tragedy of *Hamlet,* as it is perhaps the chief tragic mystery of life . . .

The imagery in *Macbeth* appears to me to be more rich and varied, more highly imaginative, more unapproachable by any other writer, than that of any other single play. It is particularly so, I think, in the continuous use made of the simplest, humblest, everyday things, drawn from the daily life in a small house, as a vehicle for sublime poetry. But that is beside our point here.

The ideas in the imagery are in themselves more imaginative, more subtle and complex than in other plays, and there are a greater number of them, interwoven the one with the other, recurring and repeating. . . .

The feeling of fear, horror and pain is increased by the constant and recurring images of blood; these are very marked, and have been noticed by others, especially by Bradley, the most terrible being Macbeth's description of himself wading in a river of blood, while the most stirring to the imagination, perhaps in the whole of Shakespeare, is the picture of him gazing, rigid with horror, at his own blood-stained hand and watching it dye the whole green ocean red.

The images of animals also, nearly all predatory, unpleasant or fierce, add to this same feeling; such are a nest of scorpions, a venomous serpent and a snake, a 'hell-kite' eating chickens, a devouring vulture, a swarm of insects, a tiger, rhinoceros and bear, the tiny wren fighting the owl for the life of her young, small birds with the fear of the net, lime, pitfall or gin, used with such bitter ironic effect by Lady Macduff and her boy just before they are murdered, the shrieking owl, and the bear tied to a stake fighting savagely to the end.

Enough has been said, I think, to indicate how complex and varied is the symbolism in the imagery of *Macbeth,* and to make it clear that an appreciable part of the emotions we feel throughout of pity, fear and horror, is due to the subtle but definite and repeated action of this imagery upon our minds, of which, in our preoccupation with the main theme, we remain often largely unconscious.

The main image in *Othello* is that of animals in action, preying upon one another, mischievous, lascivious, cruel or suffering, and through these, the general sense of pain and unpleasantness is much increased and kept constantly before us.

More than half the animal images in the play are Iago's, and all these are contemptuous or repellent: a plague of flies, a quarrelsome dog, the recurrent image of bird-snaring, leading asses by the nose, a spider catching a fly, beating an offenceless dog, wild cats, wolves, goats and monkeys.

To these, Othello adds his pictures of foul toads breeding in a cistern, summer flies in the shambles, the ill-boding raven over the infected house, a toad in a dungeon, the monster 'too hideous to be shown', bird-snaring again, aspics' tongues, crocodiles' tears, and his reiteration of 'goats and monkeys'. In addition, Lodovico very suitably calls Iago 'that viper', and the green-eyed monster 'begot upon itself, born on itself', is described or referred to by Iago, Emilia and Desdemona. . . .

The intensity of feeling and emotion in *King Lear* and the sharpness of its focus are revealed by the fact that in Shakespeare's imagination there runs throughout only one overpowering and dominating continuous image. So compelling is this that even well-marked different and subsidiary images are pressed into its service, and used to augment and emphasise it.

In the play we are conscious all through of the atmosphere of buffeting, strain and strife, and, at moments, of bodily tension to the point of agony. So naturally does this flow from the circumstances of the drama and the mental sufferings of Lear, that we scarcely realise how greatly this sensation in us is increased by the general 'floating' image, kept constantly before us, chiefly by means of the verbs used, but also in metaphor, of a human body in anguished movement, tugged, wrenched, beaten, pierced, stung, scourged, dislocated, flayed, gashed, scalded, tortured and finally broken on the rack. . . .

Through all the tragedies I have now traced the recurring images which serve as 'motifs' in the plays. My analysis is perhaps sufficient to show how definite and how potent are these images within images, and how profoundly we are influenced by the emotional background which they call into being. No other writer, so far as I know, certainly no other dramatist, makes such continual use of the running and recurrent symbol as does Shakespeare. Shelley, in his *Prometheus Unbound*, perhaps comes nearest to it, when he brings out and emphasises, by means of his nature imagery, certain philosophical and ethical thoughts; but the *Prometheus*, though nominally a drama, is really a lyrical poem in a single mood, which lends itself far more readily to such continuity of symbolism than do Shakespeare's varied and tremendous dramas.

This method of working by way of suggestion, springing from a succession of vivid pictures and concrete details, is, of course, of the very essence of 'romantic' art; and, in the case of Shakespeare, the poet's mind, unlike the dyer's hand, subdues to itself what it works in, and colours with its dominating emotion all the varied material which comes its way, colours it so subtly and so delicately that for the most part we are unconscious of what is happening, and know only the total result of the effect on our imaginative sensibility.

Hence it seems to me that a study of Shakespeare's imagery from the angle from which we have been looking at it in the latter part of this book helps us to realise a little more fully and accurately one of the many ways by which he so magically stirs our emotions and excites our imagination. I believe it not only does this, but sometimes even throws a fresh ray of light on the significance of the play concerned, and – most important of all – on the way Shakespeare himself saw it.

J. I. M. Stewart
Character and Motive in Shakespeare (1949)

The classical line of Shakespearean interpretation through character is defended against the 'realistic' school of historical criticism in this influential critical reaction; the need to modify Bradley is accepted, and character is seen in its relation to theatre and poetry in a sanely balanced approach to Shakespearean tragedy.

If we seek through the many phases of Shakespeare criticism for some cardinal assertion in the truth of which most great names in every century concur we shall arrive, I think, at this: Shakespeare understood the passions and described, or conveyed, their several and conjoined operations with certainty, subtlety and power. It is the opinion of Dryden, the father of our criticism and a dramatist having good cause to discriminate men and dummies; of Johnson, a moralist ceaselessly curious in conduct and the best of Shakespeare's comprehensive critics; of Coleridge of the dispersed and incomparable perceptions; of Andrew Bradley, whose book is at once so lucid and so profound; and of Sigmund Freud, who distinguished in the plays a regular consonance with the radical workings of the minds of real men and women. Here, one may fairly claim, is the classical line in Shakespeare criticism, and those who would depart from it must show their credentials. Some of these credentials I shall do my best to examine in the present book.

It would be foolish to deny the bracing influence which historical and comparative method has had upon the aesthetic criticism of Shakespeare, or the need for many modifications of our received opinions which recent scholarship has exposed. I am far from thinking that *Shakespearean Tragedy*, for example, can continue to stand without qualification in face of such researches as Professor Elmer Edgar Stoll's. But I believe that the 'realists' (as they have come to be called) are mistaken on the whole in the emphasis of their criticism, and that if they do indeed sometimes show that there is less in the plays than Bradley supposes, yet inquiries in quite other fields powerfully suggest that there is more - more, I mean, of that insight into the 'obscurer regions of man's being' which Bradley asserts and which the realists are inclined to deny. . . .

The characters, then (but I mean chiefly those major characters with whom the imagination of the dramatist is deeply engaged), have often the superior reality of individuals exposing the deepest springs of their action. But this superior reality is manifested through the medium of situations which are sometimes essentially symbolical; and these may be extravagant or merely fantastic when not interpreted by the quickened imagination, for it is only during the prevalence of a special mode of consciousness, the poetic, that the underlying significance of these situations is perceived. Moreover powerful forces - the mandates of our culture - stand ready here to step in with a sort of censorship when they can. This is why, in Mr. Wilson Knight's phrase, 'the memory will always try to reject the imagination.'

If it is the medium of poetic drama that permits the use of symbolic or expressionist devices in what remains nevertheless the presentation of true and indeed profound psychological perceptions, it must follow that in the modern neglect of the medium - whether through pedestrian or inadequate imaginative reading, or through the tradition of performing the plays with as much business and spectacle and as little poetry as possible – there must lie a further occasion for depreciating the truth of Shakespearean character. And it is when the poetic drama is no longer with any certainty read poetically that the way is opened for such vagaries of historical criticism as I am to discuss. Communication has become muted or imperfect and the critic senses this. He takes the play from the shelf and cannot discern or decide what is really there. So what, he asks, is *likely* to be there? Criticism holds no more fatal question . . .

Shakespeare's characters – this character and that character – often have far more 'psychology' than historical realism would suppose. And, in so far as this holds, Shakespeare's drama is naturalistic in a simple, if not in the simplest, signification: it gives individuals as a profoundly intuitive mind is aware of them. But perhaps none of Shakespeare's great plays is merely naturalistic in this sense; and he does freely use characters like Iago who have at times, and as independent beings, no more psychology than Stoll is prepared to allow them. Nevertheless these characters are composed into a whole which, I think, has psychology, or which is in the total impression an image of life. Iago is unreal, and Stoll is right about him. Othello is unreal, and Stoll is right about him also. But the two together and in interaction are not unreal. The two together make your mind, or mine.

Clifford Leech
Shakespeare's Tragedies (1950)

Modern theories of tragedy have argued that the cathartic effect of Aristotle is achieved by a balance of forces; for I. A. Richards it was the balance between the emotions of pity and fear; for Una Ellis-Fermor the opposition between a sense of an alien and hostile destiny and a view that an apparent evil could be explained in terms of a controlling force for good. Leech in his approach to Shakespearean tragedy offers the explanation of a sense of balance between terror and pride. He notes the closeness to the everyday world of Elizabethan tragedy as compared with Greek tragedy; the Shakespearean tragic hero is set in a pre-ordained pattern of events, but there is a greater sense of individual free will than in the compelling inevitability of the classical Greek play.

In such a world-picture as the tragic writer presents to us, it may appear difficult to see how an equilibrium of forces can exist. The impact on our minds of such inhuman justice would at first sight appear only terrible and paralysing. Yet it remains true that our experience of tragic drama is not like that. When we think of Shakespeare's tragedies, of Webster's, of Marlowe's, or of modern tragedies like Mr. Eugene O'Neill's *Mourning Becomes Electra*, or of Mr. Sean O'Casey's *Juno and the Paycock*, what we recall is made up of an indifferent universe and certain characters who seem to demand our admiration. Whether the characters are comparatively blameless, like Hamlet or Webster's Duchess, or deeply guilty, like Macbeth, we feel that they have a quality of mind that somehow atones for the nature of the world in which they and we live. They have, in a greater or lesser degree, the power to endure and the power to apprehend; ultimately they are destroyed, but in all their sufferings they show an increasing readiness to endure, an even greater awareness. As the shadows gather around them, they stand up the more resolutely, they see the human situation with clearer eyes. Webster's Duchess is at the beginning of the play merely an attractive and enterprising woman, but it is when she cries, in the midst of torment: 'I am Duchess of Malfi still,' that we recognize her full stature. Lear develops even more remarkably from a vain, hot-tempered tyrant to a man who sees the omnipresence of social wrong and the bodily distress of the poor. So, too, our attitude to Electra and Orestes and Oedipus is inevitably one of growing admiration. Because, moreover, the dramatist has made it clear that his tragic hero is human, a man with weaknesses like our own, we feel not merely admiration but pride: we are proud of our human nature because in such characters it comes to fine flower. In a planned but terrible universe we see man justifying his existence.

Thus the equilibrium of tragedy consists in a balancing of Terror with Pride. On the one hand, we are impelled to withdraw from the spectacle, to try to forget the revelation of evil methodised; on the other, we are aroused to withstand destiny, to strive to meet it with the fortitude and the clear eyes of the tragic figure. This feeling of Pride comes into full existence when the hero knows his fate and contemplates it: it is essentially distinct from the *hubris* which he may display, but which we cannot share in, before his eyes are opened.

The tragic picture of the universe postulates a limited free will. Man cannot determine the pattern of events, but he is frequently responsible either for the initiation of an evil chain or for the release of evil forces latent in a situation. Moreover, his thoughts and feelings, his attitude to the enveloping situation, are in his own control: like Orestes, he can see the horror of the matricide he must commit; like Macbeth, he can recognize his own weakness and ultimately his own insignificance in the universal scheme. Some degree of free will is, indeed, essential in tragedy, for we could hardly feel proud of an automaton.

Because of its closer approximation to the everyday appearance of things, there seems to be a greater degree of free will in Elizabethan than in Greek tragedy: it seems as if Hamlet could deflect the course of the action at almost any point if he wished, while clearly Orestes and Oedipus are bound to an established pattern. But Shakespeare and his contemporaries have gone out of their way to make us realise that the pattern is preordained for their characters too: in some plays Shakespeare uses supernatural devices to indicate the course of future events – for example in *Macbeth, Julius Caesar* and *Antony and Cleopatra* – and always he draws his characters in such a way that there is clearly only one line of conduct possible for them in the particular situation in which they find themselves: for them it is the doom-in-the-character rather than the doom-on-the-house. Hamlet must be killed because Hamlet in his particular situation can have no other end: his fate is as inevitable as that of man lost in the heart of a desert.

3

Critics and the 'great' tragedies

HAMLET (1600–1601)

Critical problems abound in this most problematical of all Shakespeare's plays, and centre on the character of Hamlet which has
fascinated commentators across the centuries. The question of
Hamlet's delay in taking his revenge, the morality of his embroilment
in the action, his relationship with the women in the play and the
ghost of his father, his madness and soliloquizing introspection,
which contrasts with the intervening precipitate action, have given
rise to an immense body of criticism. Romantic enthusiasm for an
idealized hero has been modified in the anti-heroic climate of the
twentieth century, but in the popular imagination it is probably still
Hamlet above all which represents the essence of Shakespearean
tragedy.

Samuel Johnson
The Plays of Shakespeare (1765)

Dr Johnson acknowledges the variety of Hamlet *and the richness of
the action in an early tribute to its stageworthiness. Classically
inspired prejudice is apparent in the complaint that Shakespeare fails
to achieve poetic justice, with characteristic moral indignation at the
treatment of Ophelia. Contemporary reaction to the humour of*

Hamlet's feigned madness may be contrasted with the post-Freudian modern preoccupation with mental states. Johnson's criticism is a useful insight into an apprehension of Hamlet *before the huge burden of criticism coloured approaches to the play.*

If the dramas of Shakespeare were to be characterized, each by the particular excellence which distinguishes it from the rest, we must allow to the tragedy of *Hamlet* the praise of variety. The incidents are so numerous, that the arguments of the play would make a long tale. The scenes are interchangeably diversified with merriment and solemnity; with merriment that includes judicious and instructive observation; and solemnity, not strained by poetical violence above the natural sentiments of man. New characters appear from time to time in continual succession, exhibiting various forms of life and particular modes of conversation. The pretended madness of Hamlet causes much mirth, the mournful distraction of Ophelia fills the heart with tenderness, and every personage produces the effect intended, from the apparition that in the first act chills the blood with horror, to the fop in the last, that exposes affectation to just contempt.

The conduct is perhaps not wholly secure against objections. The action is indeed for the most part in continual progression, but there are some scenes which neither forward nor retard it. Of the feigned madness of Hamlet there appears no adequate cause, for he does nothing which he might not have done with the reputation of sanity. He plays the madman most, when he treats Ophelia with so much rudeness, which seems to be useless and wanton cruelty.

Hamlet is, through the whole play, rather an instrument than an agent. After he has, by the stratagem of the play, convicted the King, he makes no attempt to punish him, and his death is at last effected by an incident which Hamlet has no part in producing.

The catastrophe is not very happily produced; the exchange of weapons is rather an expedient of necessity, than a stroke of art. A scheme might easily have been formed, to kill Hamlet with the dagger, and Laertes with the bowl.

The poet is accused of having shown little regard to poetical justice, and may be charged with equal neglect of poetical probability. The apparition left the regions of the dead to little purpose; the revenge which he demands is not obtained but by the death of him that was required to take it; and the gratification, which would arise from the destruction of an usurper and murderer, is abated by the untimely death of Ophelia, the young, the beautiful, the harmless, and the pious.

Charles Lamb
On the Tragedies of Shakespeare (1811)

This is an early witness that Hamlet had become a popular role for actors, and an endorsement of the theatrical appeal of the play. It is not in fact a denial of the actor's right to represent Hamlet that exercises Lamb, but the conviction that a true insight into the character, its solitary musings and intellectual power, can only be gained by the receptive reader. At the extreme this line of criticism could lead to the extrapolation of character from dramatic context, but can also be seen as an argument against unsuitable acting and theatrical production. Modern critics who dismiss Lamb's distrust of performance are apt to forget that they bring a direct knowledge of the text into the theatre.

The character of Hamlet is perhaps that by which, since the days of Betterton, a succession of popular performers have had the greatest ambition to distinguish themselves. The length of the part may be one of their reasons. But for the character itself, we find it in a play, and therefore we judge of it a fit subject of dramatic representation. The play itself abounds in maxims and reflexions beyond any other, and therefore we consider it as a proper vehicle for conveying moral instruction. But Hamlet himself – what does he suffer meanwhile by being dragged forth as a public schoolmaster, to give lectures to the crowd! Why, nine parts in ten of what Hamlet does, are transactions between himself and his moral sense, they are the effusions of his solitary musings, which he retires to holes and corners and the most sequestered parts of the palace to pour forth; or rather, they are the silent meditations with which his bosom is bursting, reduced to *words* for the sake of the reader, who must else remain ignorant of what is passing there. These profound sorrows, these light-and-noise-abhorring ruminations, which the tongue scarce dares utter to deaf walls and chambers, how can they be represented by a gesticulating actor, who comes and mouths them out before an audience, making four hundred people his confidants at once? I say not that it is the fault of the actor so to do; he must pronounce them *ore rotundo*, he must accompany them with his eye, he must insinuate them into his auditory by some trick of eye, tone, or gesture, or he fails. *He must be thinking all the while of his appearance, because he knows that all the while the spectators are judging of it.* And this is the way to represent the shy, negligent, retiring Hamlet.

It is true that there is no other mode of conveying a vast quantity of thought and feeling to a great portion of the audience, who otherwise would never earn it for themselves by reading, and the intellectual acquisition gained this way may, for aught I know, be inestimable; but I am not arguing that Hamlet should not be acted, but how much Hamlet is made another thing by being acted. I have heard much of the wonders which Garrick performed in this part; but as I never saw him, I must have leave to doubt whether the representation of such a character came within the province of his art. Those who tell me of him, speak of his eye, and of his commanding voice: physical properties, vastly desirable in an actor, and without which he can never insinuate meaning into an auditory, – but what have they to do with Hamlet? what have they to do with intellect? In fact, the things aimed at in theatrical representation, are to arrest the spectator's eye upon the form and gesture, and so to gain a more favourable hearing to what is spoken: it is not what the character is, but how he looks; not what he says, but how he speaks it. I see no reason to think that if the play of *Hamlet* were written over again by some such writer as Banks or Lillo, retaining the process of the story, but totally omitting all the poetry of it, all the divine features of Shakespeare, his stupendous intellect; and only taking care to give us enough of passionate dialogue, which Banks or Lillo were never at a loss to furnish; I see not how the effect could be much different upon an audience, nor how the actor has it in his power to represent Shakespeare to us differently from his representation of Banks or Lillo. Hamlet would still be a youthful accomplished prince, and must be gracefully personated; he might be puzzled in his mind, wavering in his conduct, seemingly cruel to Ophelia, he might see a ghost, and start at it, and address it kindly when he found it to be his father; all this in the poorest and most homely language of the servilest creeper after nature that ever consulted the palate of an audience; without troubling Shakespeare for the matter: and I see not but there would be room for all the power which an actor has, to display itself. All the passions and changes of passion might remain: for these are much less difficult to write or act than is thought, it is a trick easy to be attained, it is but rising or falling a note or two in the voice, a whisper with a significant foreboding look to announce its approach, and so contagious the counterfeit appearance of any emotion is, that let the words be what they will, the look and tone shall carry it off and make it pass for deep skill in the passions . . .

To return to Hamlet. – Among the distinguishing features of that wonderful character, one of the most interesting (yet painful) is that soreness of mind which makes him treat the intrusions of Polonius with harshness, and that asperity which he puts on in his interviews with Ophelia. These tokens of an unhinged mind (if they be not mixed in the latter case with a profound artifice of love, to alienate Ophelia by affected discourtesies, so to prepare her mind for the breaking off of that loving intercourse, which can no longer find a place amidst business so serious as that which he has to do) are parts of his character, which to reconcile with our admiration of Hamlet, the most patient consideration of his situation is no more than necessary; they are what we *forgive afterwards*, and explain by the whole of his character, but *at the time* they are harsh and unpleasant. Yet such is the actor's necessity of giving strong blows to the audience, that I have never seen a player in this character, who did not exaggerate and strain to the utmost these ambiguous features, – these temporary deformities in the character. They make him express a vulgar scorn at Polonius which utterly degrades his gentility, and which no explanation can render palatable; they make him shew contempt, and curl up the nose at Ophelia's father, – contempt in its very grossest and most hateful form; but they get applause by it: it is natural, people say; that is, the words are scornful, and the actor expresses scorn, and that they can judge of: but why so much scorn, and of that sort, they never think of asking.

So to Ophelia. All the Hamlets that I have ever seen, rant and rave at her as if she had committed some great crime, and the audience are highly pleased, because the words of the part are satirical, and they are enforced by the strongest expression of satirical indignation of which the face and voice are capable. But then, whether Hamlet is likely to have put on such brutal appearance to a lady whom he loved so dearly, is never thought on. The truth is, that in all such deep affections as had subsisted between Hamlet and Ophelia, there is a stock of *supererogatory love*, (if I may venture to use the expression) which in any great grief of heart, especially where that which preys upon the mind cannot be communicated, confers a kind of indulgence upon the grieved party to express itself, even to its heart's dearest object in the language of a temporary alienation; but it is not alienation, it is a distraction purely, and so it always makes itself to be felt by that object: it is not anger, but grief assuming the appearance of anger, – love awkwardly counterfeiting hate, as sweet countenances when they try to frown: but such sternness and fierce disgust as Hamlet is made to shew, is no counterfeit, but the real face of absolute aversion, – of irreconcilable alienation. It may be said he puts on the madman; but then he should only so far put on this counterfeit lunacy as his own real distraction will give him leave; that is, incompletely, imperfectly; not in that conformed, practised way, like a master of his art, or as Dame Quickly would say, 'like one of those harlotry players.'

William Hazlitt
'Characters of Shakespeare's Plays' (1817)

Like Charles Lamb, Hazlitt did not like to see Shakespeare's plays acted, 'least of all Hamlet'. *He asserts the universality of Hamlet's appeal, and the ease with which the reader identifies with the character; in this way, he acknowledges the cathartic appeal of the tragedy. Even in Hazlitt's time the sheer familiarity of the play made criticism difficult. If Hamlet is for Hazlitt the great moralizer, he sees the morality as subtly drawn from human experience, not as an opportunity for pedantry. The uniqueness of Hamlet's fascination is, as for Coleridge, to be found in the combination of fineness of thought and infirmity of action. This interpretation of Hamlet, and the stress on the 'reality' of the character, was to become the substance of much critical debate.*

This is that Hamlet the Dane, whom we read of in our youth, and whom we may be said almost to remember in our after-years; he who made that famous soliloquy on life, who gave the advice to the players, who thought 'this goodly frame, the earth, a steril promontory, and this brave o'er-hanging firmament, the air, this majestical roof fretted with golden fire, a foul and pestilent congregation of vapours;' whom 'man delighted not, nor woman neither;' he who talked with the gravediggers, and moralised on Yorick's skull; the schoolfellow of Rosencrantz and Guildenstern at Wittenberg; the friend of Horatio; the lover of Ophelia; he that was mad and sent to England; the slow avenger of his father's death; who lived at the court of Horwendillus five hundred years before we were born, but all whose thoughts we seem to know as well as we do our own, because we have read them in Shakespeare.

Hamlet is a name; his speeches and sayings but the idle coinage of the poet's brain. What then, are they not real? They are as real as our own thoughts. Their reality is in the reader's mind. It is *we* who are Hamlet. The play has a prophetic truth, which is above that of history. Whoever has become thoughtful and melancholy through his own mishaps or those of others; whoever has borne about him the clouded brow of reflection, and thought himself 'too much i' th' sun;' whoever has seen the golden lamp of day dimmed by envious mists rising in his own breast, and could find in the world before him only a dull blank with nothing left remarkable in it; whoever has known 'the pangs of despised love, the insolence of office, or the spurns which patient merit of the unworthy takes;' he who has felt his mind sink within him, and sadness cling to his heart like a malady, who has had his hopes blighted and his youth staggered by the apparitions of strange things; who cannot be well at ease, while he sees evil hovering near him like a spectre; whose powers of action have been eaten up by thought, he to whom the universe seems infinite, and himself nothing; whose bitterness of soul makes him careless of consequences, and who goes to a play as his best resource to shove off, to a second remove, the evils of life by a mock representation of them – this is the true Hamlet.

We have been so used to this tragedy that we hardly know how to criticise it any more than we should know how to describe our own faces. But we must make such observations as we can. It is the one of Shakespeare's plays that we think of the oftenest, because it abounds most in striking reflections on human life, and because the distresses of Hamlet are transferred, by the turn of his mind, to the general account of humanity. Whatever happens to him we apply to ourselves, because he applies it to himself as a means of general reasoning. He is a great moraliser; and what makes him worth attending to is, that he moralises on his own feelings and experience. He is not a common-place pedant. If *Lear* is distinguished by the greatest depth of passion, *Hamlet* is the most remarkable for the ingenuity, originality, and unstudied development of character. Shakespeare has more magnanimity than any other poet, and he has shown more of it in this play than in any other. There is no attempt to force an interest: every thing is left for time and circumstances to unfold. The attention is excited without effort, the incidents succeed each other as matters of course, the characters think and speak and act just as they might do, if left entirely to themselves. There is no set purpose, no straining at a point. The observations are suggested by the passing scene; the gusts of passion come and go like sounds of music borne on the wind. The whole play is an exact transcript of what might be supposed to have taken place at the court of Denmark, at the remote period of time fixed upon, before the modern refinements in morals and manners were heard of. It would have been interesting enough to have been admitted as a bystander in such a scene, at such a time, to have heard and witnessed something of what was going on. But here we are more than spectators. We have not only 'the outward pageants and the signs of grief;' but 'we have that within which passes shew.' We read the thoughts of the heart, we catch the passions of living as they rise. Other dramatic writers give us very fine versions and paraphrases of nature; but Shakespeare, together with his own comments, gives us the original text, that we may judge for ourselves. This is a very great advantage.

The character of Hamlet stands quite by itself. It is not a character marked by strength of will or even of passion, but by refinement of thought and sentiment. Hamlet is as little of the hero as a man can well be: but he is a young and princely novice, full of high enthusiasm and quick sensibility – the sport of circumstances, questioning with fortune and refining on his own feelings, and forced from the natural bias of his disposition by the strangeness of his situation. He seems incapable of deliberate action, and is only hurried into extremities on the spur of the occasion, when he has no time to reflect, as in the scene where he kills Polonius, and again, where he alters the letters which Rosencrantz and Guildenstern are taking with them to England, purporting his death. At other times when he is most bound to act, he remains puzzled, and undecided, and sceptical, dallies with his purposes, till the occasion is lost, and finds out some pretence to relapse into indolence and thoughtfulness again. . . .

His ruling passion is to think, not to act: and any vague pretext that flatters this propensity instantly diverts him from his previous purposes.

Samuel Taylor Coleridge
Lectures on Shakespeare (1818)

It was the character of Hamlet on which Coleridge first exercised his 'turn for philosophical criticism', and through which he sought insight into Shakespeare's genius. Coleridge acknowledges the universal fascination with the character of Hamlet, and sees Shakespeare's compelling portrayal as an ideal opportunity for investigating the operation of the human thought-processes. In this famous criticism, which was to set the tone for approaches to Hamlet *for many years, Coleridge sees in Hamlet excessive intellectual activity which leads to an aversion to physical action and hence the delay in proceeding to his revenge. Unlike some commentators, Coleridge does set Hamlet in dramatic context in his notes on the final act of the tragedy, in which Hamlet receives his summation.*

The seeming inconsistencies in the conduct and character of Hamlet have long exercised the conjectural ingenuity of critics; and, as we are always loth to suppose that the cause of defective apprehension is in ourselves, the mystery has been too commonly explained by the very easy process of setting it down as in fact inexplicable, and by resolving the phenomenon into a misgrowth or *lusus* of the capricious and irregular genius of Shakespeare. The shallow and stupid arrogance of these vulgar and indolent decisions I would fain do my best to expose. I believe the character of Hamlet may be traced to Shakespeare's deep and accurate science in mental philosophy. Indeed, that this character must have some connection with the common fundamental laws of our nature may be assumed from the fact, that Hamlet has been the darling of every country in which the literature of England has been fostered. In order to understand him, it is essential that we should reflect on the constitution of our own minds. Man is distinguished from the brute animals in proportion as thought prevails over sense: but in the healthy processes of the mind, a balance is constantly maintained between the impressions from outward objects and the inward operations of the intellect; – for if there be an overbalance in the contemplative faculty, man thereby becomes the creature of mere meditation, and loses his natural power of action. Now one of Shakespeare's modes of creating characters is, to conceive any one intellectual or moral faculty in morbid excess, and then to place himself, Shakespeare, thus mutilated or diseased, under given circumstances. In Hamlet he seems to have wished to exemplify the moral necessity of a due balance between our attention to the objects of our senses, and our meditation on the workings of our minds, – an *equilibrium* between the real and the imaginary worlds. In Hamlet this balance is disturbed: his thoughts, and the images of his fancy, are far more vivid than his actual perceptions, and his very perceptions, instantly passing through the *medium* of his contemplations, acquire, as they pass, a form and colour not naturally their own. Hence we see a great, an almost enormous, intellectual activity, and a proportionate aversion to real action, consequent upon it, with all its symptoms and accompanying qualities. This character Shakespeare places in circumstances, under which it is obliged to act on the spur of the moment: – Hamlet is brave and careless of death; but he vacillates from sensibility, and procrastinates from thought, and loses the power of action in the energy of resolve. Thus it is that this tragedy presents a direct contrast to that of Macbeth; the one proceeds with the utmost slowness, the other with a crowded and breathless rapidity.

The effect of this overbalance of the imaginative power is beautifully illustrated in the everlasting broodings and superfluous activities of Hamlet's mind, which, unseated from its healthy relation, is constantly occupied with the world within, and abstracted from the world without, – giving substance to shadows, and throwing a mist over all commonplace actualities. It is the nature of thought to be indefinite; – definiteness belongs to external imagery alone. Hence it is that the sense of sublimity arises, not from the sight of an outward object, but from the beholder's reflection upon it; – not from the sensuous impression, but from the imaginative reflex. Few have seen a celebrated waterfall without feeling something akin to disappointment: it is only subsequently that the image comes back full into the mind, and brings with it a train of grand or beautiful associations. Hamlet feels this; his senses are in a state of trance, and he looks upon external things as hieroglyphics. His soliloquy –

O ! that this too too solid flesh would melt &c.

springs from that craving after the indefinite – for that which is not – which most easily besets men of genius; and the self-delusion common to this temper of mind is finely exemplified in the character which Hamlet gives of himself:

- It cannot be
But I am pigeon-livered, and lack gall
To make oppression bitter.

He mistakes the seeing his chains for the breaking of them, delays till action is of no use, and dies the victim of mere circumstance and accident. . . .

O, the rich contrast between the Clowns and Hamlet, as two extremes! You see in the former the mockery of logic and a traditional wit valued, like truth, for its antiquity, and treasured up, like a tune, for use.

Shakespeare seems to mean all Hamlet's character to be brought together before his final disappearance from the scene; – his meditative excess in the grave-digging, his yielding to passion with Laertes, his love for Ophelia blazing out, his tendency to generalize on all occasions in the dialogue with Horatio, his fine gentlemanly manners with Osrick, and his and Shakespeare's own fondness for presentiment:

> But thou would'st not think, how ill all's here about my heart: but it is no matter.

A. C. Bradley
Shakespearean Tragedy (1904)

Bradley acknowledges Hamlet *as the most popular of Shakespeare's plays, and applies psychological realism to the analysis of Hamlet's character in his approach to the tragedy. That Hamlet's delay in taking revenge is because of external factors, or because of an excess of conscience, he completely dismisses. The Romantic, sentimental, view of Hamlet, summed up by Goethe's famous description of 'a lovely, pure and most moral nature', who lacks heroic nerve and cannot shoulder his burden, Bradley rejects as reducing the tragedy to mere pathos. He addresses the most widely supported view, the Schlegel – Coleridge argument that sees* Hamlet *as a tragedy of reflection, with particular care, but offers instead the explanation of Hamlet's profound melancholy. The detailed argument does not ignore the dramatic context, although it sees the psychological explanation of the hero as the only approach to the tragedy and the key to understanding its greatness.*

There remains, finally, that class of view which may be named after Schlegel and Coleridge. According to this, *Hamlet*, is the tragedy of reflection. The cause of the hero's delay is irresolution; and the cause of this irresolution is excess of the reflective or speculative habit of mind. He has a general intention to obey the Ghost, but 'the native hue of resolution is sicklied o'er with pale cast of thought.' He is 'thought sick'. 'The whole', says Schlegel, 'is intended to show how a calculating consideration which aims at exhausting, so far as human foresight can, all the relations and possible consequences of a deed, cripples the power of acting ... Hamlet is a hypocrite towards himself; his far-fetched scruples are often mere pretexts to cover his want of determination ... He has no firm belief in himself or in anything else ... He loses himself in labyrinths of thought.' So Coleridge finds in Hamlet 'an almost enormous intellectual activity and a proportionate aversion to real action consequent on the activity' (the aversion, that is to say, is consequent on the activity). Professor Dowden objects to this view, very justly, that it neglects the emotional side of Hamlet's character, 'which is quite as important as the intellectual'; but, with this supplement, he appears on the whole to adopt it. Hamlet, he says, 'loses a sense of fact because with him each object and event transforms and expands itself into an idea ... He cannot steadily keep alive within himself a sense of the importance of any positive, limited thing, – a deed, for example.' And Professor Dowden explains this condition by reference to Hamlet's life. 'When the play opens he has reached the age of thirty years ... and he has received culture of every kind except the culture of active life. During the reign of the strong-willed elder Hamlet there was no call to action for his meditative son. He has slipped on into years of full manhood still a haunter of the university, a student of philosophies, an amateur in art, a ponderer on the things of life and death, who has never formed a resolution or executed a deed.'

On the whole, the Schlegel–Coleridge theory (with or without Professor Dowden's modification and amplification) is the most widely received view of Hamlet's character. And with it we come at last into close contact with the text of the play. It not only answers, in some fundamental respects, to the general impression produced by the drama, but it can be supported by Hamlet's own words in his soliloquys – such words, for example, as those about native hue of resolution, or those about the craven scruple of thinking too precisely on the event. It is confirmed, also, by the contrast between Hamlet on the one side and Laertes and Fortinbras on the other; and, further, by the occurrence of those words of the King to Laertes (IV. vii. 119 f) which, if they are not in character, are all the more important as showing what was in Shakespeare's mind at the time:

> that we would do
> We should do when we would; for this 'would' changes,
> And hath abatements and delays as many

As there are tongues, are hands, are accidents;
And then this 'should' is like a spendthrift sigh
That hurts by easing.

And, lastly, even if the view itself does not suffice, the *description* given by its adherents of Hamlet's state of mind, as we see him in the last four Acts, is, on the whole and so far as it goes, a true description. The energy or resolve is dissipated in an endless brooding on the deed required. When he acts, his action does not proceed from this deliberation and analysis, but is sudden and impulsive, evoked by an emergency in which he has no time to think. And most of the reasons he assigns for his procrastination are evidently not the true reasons, but unconscious excuses.

Nevertheless this theory fails to satisfy. And it fails, not merely in this or that detail, but as a whole. We feel that its Hamlet does not fully answer to our imaginative impression. He is not nearly so inadequate to this impression as the sentimental Hamlet, but still we feel he is inferior to Shakespeare's man and does him wrong. And when we come to examine the theory we find that it is partial and leaves much unexplained. I pass that by for the present, for we shall see, I believe, that the theory is also positively misleading, and that in a most important way. And of this I propose to speak.

Hamlet's irresolution, or his aversion to real action, is, according to the theory, the *direct* result of 'an almost enormous intellectual activity' in the way of 'a calculating consideration which attempts to exhaust all the relations and possible consequences of a deed.' And this again proceeds from an original one-sidedness of nature, strengthened by habit, and, perhaps, by years of speculative inaction. The theory describes, therefore, a man in certain respects like Coleridge himself, on one side a man of genius, on the other side, the side of will, deplorably weak, always procrastinating and avoiding unpleasant duties, and often reproaching himself in vain; a man, observe, who at *any* time and in *any* circumstances would be unequal to the task assigned to Hamlet. And thus, I must maintain, it degrades Hamlet, and travesties the play. For Hamlet, according to all the indications in the text, was not naturally or normally such a man, but rather, I venture to affirm, a man who at any *other* time and in any *other* circumstances than those presented would have been perfectly equal to his task; and it is, in fact, the very cruelty of his fate that the crisis of his life comes on him at the one moment when he cannot meet it, and when his highest gifts, instead of helping him, conspire to paralyse him. This aspect of the tragedy the theory quite misses; and it does so because it misconceives the cause of that irresolution which, on the whole, it truly describes. For the cause was not directly or mainly an habitual excess of reflectiveness. The direct cause was a state of mind quite abnormal and induced by special circumstances, – a state of profound melancholy. Now, Hamlet's reflectiveness doubtless played a certain part in the *production* of that melancholy, and was thus one indirect contributory cause of his irresolution. And, again, the melancholy, once established, displayed, as one of its *symptoms*, an excessive reflection on the required deed. But excess of reflection was not, as the theory makes it, the *direct* cause of the irresolution at all; nor was it the *only* indirect cause; and in the Hamlet of the last four Acts it is to be considered rather a symptom of his state than a cause of it. . . .

I have dwelt thus at length on Hamlet's melancholy because, from the psychological point of view, it is the centre of the tragedy, and to omit it from consideration or to underrate its intensity is to make Shakespeare's story unintelligible. But the psychological point of view is not equivalent to the tragic; and, having once given its due weight to the fact of Hamlet's melancholy, we may freely admit, or rather may be anxious to insist, that this pathological condition would excite but little, if any, tragic interest if it were not the condition of a nature distinguished by that speculative genius on which the Schlegel-Coleridge type of theory lays stress. Such theories misinterpret the connection between that genius and Hamlet's failure, but still it is this connection which gives to his story its peculiar fascination and makes it appear (if the phrase may be allowed) as the symbol of a tragic mystery inherent in human nature. Wherever this mystery touches us, wherever we are forced to feel the wonder and awe of man's god-like 'apprehension' and his 'thoughts that wander through eternity,' and at the same time are forced to see him powerless in his petty sphere of action, and powerless (it would appear) from the very divinity of his thought, we remember Hamlet. And this is the reason why, in the great ideal movement which began towards the close of the eighteenth century, this tragedy acquired a position unique among Shakespeare's drama, and shared only by Goethe's *Faust*. It was not that *Hamlet* is Shakespeare's greatest tragedy or most perfect work of art; it was that *Hamlet* most brings home to us at once the sense of the soul's infinity, and the sense of the doom which not only circumscribes that infinity but appears to be its offspring.

J. Dover Wilson
What Happens in Hamlet (1935)

Psychological realism applied to Hamlet *reached the world of psychiatry itself with Dr Ernest Jones's diagnosis of Freud's 'Oedipus Complex' to account for Hamlet's ambivalent state of mind. Tension between conscious and repressed subconscious desires, clinically labelled a psychoneurosis, provides an alluring explanation of the Hamlet-Gertrude-Ophelia-Claudius relationship. Scientific explanation replaces critical preoccupation with a situation which, Dr Jones handsomely recognized, 'the genius of Shakespeare depicted . . . with faultless insight'. Representing a widespread critical reaction to this medical incursion, Dover Wilson rejects the treatment of Hamlet as a clinical case-history, with a firm reminder that* Hamlet *is drama, not history. That Hamlet is labouring under mental stress is accepted, but his spiritual triumph is the corollary. The importance in the critical approach is not psychological explication or consistency, but the sense of doubt and wonder at the mystery which is at the heart of this great tragedy.*

We are driven, therefore, to conclude with Loening, Bradley, Clutton-Brock and other critics that Shakespeare meant us to imagine Hamlet suffering from some kind of mental disorder throughout the play. Directly, however, such critics begin trying to define the exact nature of the disorder, they go astray. Its immediate origin cannot be questioned; it is caused, as we have seen, by the burden which fate lays upon his shoulders. We are not, however, at liberty to go outside the frame of the play and seek remoter origins in his past history. It is now well known, for instance, that a breakdown like Hamlet's is often due to seeds of disturbance planted in infancy and brought to evil fruition under the influence of mental strain of some kind in later life. Had Shakespeare been composing *Hamlet* today, he might conceivably have given us a hint of such an infantile complex. But he knew nothing of these matters and to write as if he did is to beat the air. We may go further. It is entirely misleading to attempt to describe Hamlet's state of mind in terms of modern psychology at all, not merely because Shakespeare did not think in these terms, but because – once again – Hamlet is a character in a play, not in history. He is part only, if the most important part, of an artistic masterpiece, of what is perhaps the most successful piece of dramatic illusion the world has ever known. And at no point of the composition is the illusion more masterly contrived than in this matter of his distraction.

In *Hamlet* Shakespeare sets out to create a hero labouring under mental infirmity, just as later in *Macbeth* he depicted a hero afflicted by moral infirmity, or in *Othello* a hero tortured by an excessive and morbid jealousy. Hamlet struggles against his weakness, and the struggle is in great measure the groundwork of his tragedy. But though he struggles in vain, and is in the end brought to disaster, a disaster largely of his own making and involving his own house and that of Polonius, we are never allowed to feel that his spirit is vanquished until 'the potent poison quite o'er-crows' it. Had he been represented as a mere madman, we should of course have felt this; he would have ceased to be a hero and, while retaining our pity, would have forfeited our sympathy, our admiration – and our censure. Ophelia exclaims,

> O, what a noble mind is here o'erthrown !

We know better: we realise that the mind is impaired, but we do not doubt for a moment that its nobility remains un-touched; we see his sovereign reason often

> Like sweet bells jangled, out of tune and harsh,

yet all the while it retains its sovereignty and can recall its sweetness. There may be contradictions here; but we are not moving in the realm of logic. From the point of view of analytic psychology such a character may even seem a monster of inconsistency. This does not matter, if as here it also seems to spectators in the theatre to be more convincingly life-like than any other character in literature. For most critics have agreed that Hamlet is one of the greatest and most fascinating of Shakespeare's creations; that he is a study in genius. Shakespeare, in short, accomplished that which he intended; he wrote a supreme tragedy. In poetic tragedy we contemplate beings greater than ourselves, greater than it is possible for man to be, enduring and brought to a calamitous end by sorrow or affliction or weakness of character which we should find unendurable; and we contemplate all this with unquestioning assent and with astonishment that deepens into awe. In the making of Hamlet, therefore, Shakespeare's task was not to produce a being psychologically explicable or consistent, but one who would evoke the affection, the wonder and the tears of his audience, and would yet be accepted as entirely human. . . .

In fine we were never intended to reach the heart of the mystery. That it has a heart is an illusion; the mystery itself is an illusion; Hamlet is an illusion. The secret that lies behind it all is not Hamlet's, but Shakespeare's: the technical devices he employed to create this supreme illusion of a great and mysterious character, who is at once mad and the sanest of geniuses, at once a procrastinator and a vigorous man of action, at once a miserable failure and the most adorable of heroes. The character of Hamlet, like the appearance of his successive impersonators on the stage, is a matter of 'make-up.' . . .

In this enquiry into the dramatic make-up of Hamlet I have been doing what, of course, Shakespeare never intended us to do: I have been peeping behind the scenes of the theatre of his imagination. The impertinence has been forced upon me by the false and, as I think, degrading notions of his art current in our time. For it is only by trying to exhibit what he attempted and how he accomplished it that one can defend him from the charges of technical incompetence and slovenliness. There is nothing slovenly in *Hamlet*, whatever may be said about some of his other plays. The more one contemplates it the more flawless and subtle does its technique appear. What, then, is the general impression which Shakespeare, by means of the devices we have been examining, strove to give of Hamlet's character? Surely it is simply the impression which three centuries of spectators (apart from critics and readers, who treat the play as a book, as a novel or a chapter of history) have always received, viz. that of a great, an almost super-human, figure tottering beneath a tragic burden too heavy even for his mighty back; or, if you will, of a genius suffering from a fatal weakness and battling against it, until in the end it involves him in the catastrophe which is at once his liberation and his atonement.

Finally, this compound of overwhelmingly convincing humanity and psychological contradiction is the greatest of Shakespeare's legacies to the men of his own quality. No 'part' in the whole repertory of dramatic literature is so certain of success with almost any audience, and is yet open to such a remarkable variety of interpretation. There are as many Hamlets as there are actors who play him; and Bernhardt has proved that even a woman can score a success. Of a role so indeterminate in composition almost any version is possible; with a character so fascinating and so tremendous in outline hardly any impersonator can fail.

OTHELLO (1604–1605)

There are several respects in which *Othello* differs markedly from the other major tragedies, and these have influenced critical approaches to the play. This is a domestic tragedy involving non-royal personages, and its principal character is black. The plot is simple and unitary, with virtually no comic relief, and the play comes the closest of the tragedies to adherence to the unities. Modern criticism has been much concerned with the 'double time' scheme – the fact that the main action of the play almost equals the passage on the stage, while the alleged adultery is implied on a different time-scale. Character evaluation for long concentrated on Iago's supposed 'motiveless malignity', with Othello's 'romantic vision' at the heart of the tragic downfall. Modern criticism has made determined attempts to downgrade Iago's importance, undermine the image of the 'noble Moor', and to question the seeming innocence of Desdemona. The emotive aspects of race and sex have complicated character evaluation; as a corollary the dramatic effectiveness of the poetry and the linguistic subtlety of Shakespeare's use of a key word like 'honest' have been highlighted.

Samuel Johnson
The Plays of Shakespeare (1765)

The scrupulous regularity of the action receives Dr Johnson's approval, as might have been predicted, although he regrets that the opening was not in Cyprus. With pre-Freudian innocence he has no doubts about Desdemona's 'soft simplicity', and he is prepared to pity the Moor as a noble victim of Iago's dark and artful malignity. The moral certainties of Johnson's interpretation seem a far·cry from modern ambivalences.

The beauties of this play impress themselves so strongly upon the attention of the reader, that they can draw no aid from critical illustration. The fiery openness of Othello, magnanimous, artless, and credulous, boundless in his confidence, ardent in his affection, inflexible in his resolution, and obdurate in his revenge; the cool malignity of Iago, silent in his resentment, subtle in his designs, and studious at once of his interest and his vengeance; the soft simplicity of Desdemona, confident of merit, and conscious of innocence, her artless perseverance in her suit, and her slowness to suspect that she can be suspected, are such proofs of Shakespeare's skill in human nature, as, I suppose, it is vain to seek in any modern writer. The gradual progress which Iago makes in the Moor's conviction, and the circumstances which he employs to enflame him, are so artfully natural, that, though it will perhaps not be said of him as he says of himself, that he is 'a man not easily jealous', yet we cannot but pity him when at last we find him 'perplexed in the extreme.'

There is always danger lest wickedness conjoined with abilities should steal upon esteem, though it misses of approbation; but the character of Iago is so conducted, that he is from the first scene to the last hated and despised.

Even the inferior characters of this play would be very conspicuous in any other piece, not only for their justness but their strength. Cassio is brave, benevolent, and honest, ruined only by his want of stubbornness to resist an insidious invitation. Roderigo's suspicious credulity, and the impatient submission to the cheats which he sees practised upon him, and which by persuasion he suffers to be repeated, exhibit a strong picture of a weak mind betrayed by unlawful desires, to a false friend; and the virtue of Aemilia is such as we often find, worn loosely, but not cast off, easy to commit small crimes, but quickened and alarmed at atrocious villainies.

The scenes from the beginning to the end are busy, varied by happy interchanges, and regularly promoting the progression of the story; and the narrative in the end, though it tells but what is known already, yet is necessary to produce the death of Othello.

Had the scene opened in Cyprus, and the preceding incidents been occasionally related, there had been little wanting to a drama of the most exact and scrupulous regularity.

Charles Lamb
On the Tragedies of Shakespeare (1811)

That Othello is black has been disputed, but accepting the fact the critical question hinges on the dramatic implications for the play and the prejudices of the beholder. Lamb appears to accept the dramatic implications of Shakespeare's deliberate choice of a black tragic hero, but voices his prejudices in resisting the starkness of the visual impact.

Lear is essentially impossible to be represented on a stage. But how many dramatic personages are there in Shakespeare, which though more tractable and feasible (if I may so speak) than Lear, yet from some circumstance, some adjunct to their character, are improper to be shewn to our bodily eye. Othello for instance. Nothing can be more soothing, more flattering to the nobler parts of our natures, than to read of a young Venetian lady of highest extraction, through the force of love and from a sense of merit in him whom she loved, laying aside every consideration of kindred, and country, and colour, and wedding with *a coal-black Moor* – (for such he is represented, in the imperfect state of knowledge respecting foreign countries in those days, compared with our own, or in compliance with popular notions, though the Moors are now well enough known to be by many shades less unworthy of a white woman's fancy) – it is the perfect triumph of virtue over accidents, of the imagination over the senses. She sees Othello's colour in his mind. But upon the stage, when the imagination is no longer the ruling faculty, but we are left to our poor unassisted senses, I appeal to every one that has seen Othello played, whether he did not, on the contrary, sink Othello's mind in his colour; whether he did not find something extremely revolting in the courtship and wedded caresses of Othello and Desdemona; and whether the actual sight of the thing did not over-weigh all that beautiful compromise which we make in reading; – and the reason it should do so is obvious, because there is just so much reality presented to our senses as to give a perception of disagreement, with not enough of belief in the internal motives, – all that which is unseen, – to overpower and reconcile the first and obvious prejudices. What we see upon a stage is body and bodily action; what we are conscious of in reading is almost exclusively the mind, and its movements: and this I think may sufficiently account for the very different sort of delight with which the same play so often affects us in the reading and the seeing.

William Hazlitt
'Characters of Shakespeare's Plays' (1817)

Like many critics, and most audiences, Hazlitt found that Othello
*'excites our sympathy to an extraordinary degree'. Of all Shakespeare's
tragedies he thought that this aroused the most intense emotional and
moral involvement. His approach through character led him to praise
its variety, and to highlight the dramatic contrast between Othello and
Iago, emphasized by their difference in colour. In contrast with
Lamb's view, Othello's blackness, embodying a true nobility, is seen as
a master-stroke of dramatic defiance of conventional prejudice. A
persistent critical theme is touched on when Hazlitt notes the
'unforeseen change' that overcomes Othello. For Hazlitt the answer to
the critical question of Iago's motivation lies in the character's love of
power. Iago's sense of intellectual superiority, stressed by many critics,
he sees as a characteristic of 'Our ancient', who manipulates those
around him as an 'amateur of tragedy'. E. E. Stoll was later to note that
the villain in Elizabethan tragedy takes the place of the ancient Fate,
or obtruding god.*

The picturesque contrasts of character in this play are almost as
remarkable as the depth of the passion. The Moor Othello, the gentle
Desdemona, the villain Iago, the good-natured Cassio, the fool
Roderigo, present a range and variety of character as striking and
palpable as that produced by the opposition of costume in a picture.
Their distinguishing qualities stand out to the mind's eye, so that even
when we are not thinking of their actions or sentiments, the idea of
their persons is still as present to us as ever. These characters and the
images they stamp upon the mind are the farthest asunder possible,
the distance between them is immense: yet the compass of knowledge
and invention which the poet has shown in embodying these extreme
creations of his genius is only greater than the truth and felicity with
which he has identified each character with itself, or blended their
different qualities together in the same story. What a contrast the
character of Othello forms to that of Iago! At the same time, the force
of conception with which these two figures are opposed to each other
is rendered still more intense by the complete consistency with which
the traits of each character are brought out in a state of the highest

finishing. The making one black and the other white, the one unprincipled, the other unfortunate in the extreme, would have answered the common purpose of effect, and satisfied the ambition of an ordinary painter of character. Shakespeare has laboured the finer shades of difference in both with as much care and skill as if he had had to depend on the execution alone for the success of his design. On the other hand, Desdemona and Aemilia are not meant to be opposed with any thing like strong contrast to each other. Both are, to outward appearance, characters of common life, not more distinguished than women usually are, by difference of rank and situation. The difference of their thoughts and sentiments is however laid open, their minds are separated from each other by signs as plain and as little to be mistaken as the complexions of their husbands.

The movement of the passion in Othello is exceedingly different from that of Macbeth. In Macbeth there is a violent struggle between opposite feelings, between ambition and the stings of conscience, almost from first to last: in Othello, the doubtful conflict between contrary passions, though dreadful, continues only for a short time, and the chief interest is excited by the alternative ascendancy of different passions, by the entire and unforeseen change from the fondest love and most unbounded confidence to the tortures of jealousy and the madness of hatred. The revenge of Othello, after it has once taken thorough possession of his mind, never quits it, but grows stronger and stronger, at every moment of its delay. The nature of the Moor is noble, confiding, tender, and generous; but his blood is of the most inflammable kind; and being once roused by a sense of his wrongs, he is stopped by no considerations of remorse or pity till he has given a loose to all the dictates of his rage and despair. It is in working his noble nature up to this extremity through rapid but gradual transitions, in raising passion to its height from the smallest beginnings and in spite of all obstacles, in painting the expiring conflict between love and hatred, tenderness and resentment, jealousy and remorse, in unfolding the strength and the weakness of our nature, in uniting sublimity of thought with the anguish of the keenest woe, in putting in motion the various impulses that agitate this our mortal being, and at last blending them in that noble tide of deep and sustained passion, impetuous but majestic, that 'flows on to the Propontic, and knows no ebb,' that Shakespeare has shown the mastery of his genius and of his power over the human heart. . . .

The character of Iago is one of the supererogations of Shakespeare's genius. Some persons, more nice than wise, have thought this whole character unnatural, because his villainy is *without a sufficient motive*.

Shakespeare, who was as good a philosopher as he was a poet, thought otherwise. He knew that the love of power, which is another name for the love of mischief, is natural to man. He would know this as well or better than if it had been demonstrated to him by a logical diagram, merely from seeing children paddle in the dirt or kill flies for sport. Iago in fact belongs to a class of character, common to Shakespeare and at the same time peculiar to him; whose heads are as acute and active as their hearts are hard and callous. Iago is to be sure an extreme instance of the kind; that is to say, of diseased intellectual activity, with the most perfect indifference to moral good or evil, or rather with a decided preference of the latter, because it falls more readily in with his favourite propensity, gives greater zest to his thoughts and scope to his actions. He is quite or nearly as indifferent to his own fate as to that of others; he runs all risks for a trifling and doubtful advantage; and is himself the dupe and victim of his ruling passion – an insatiable craving after action of the most difficult and dangerous kind. 'Our ancient' is a philosopher, who fancies that a lie that kills has more point in it than an alliteration or an antithesis; who thinks a fatal experiment on the peace of a family a better thing than watching the palpitations in the heart of a flea in a microscope; who plots the ruin of his friends as an exercise for his ingenuity, and stabs men in the dark to prevent *ennui*. His gaiety, such as it is, arises from the success of his treachery; his ease from the torture he has inflicted on others. He is an amateur of tragedy in real life; and instead of employing his invention on imaginary characters, or long-forgotten incidents, he takes the bolder and more desperate course of getting up his plot at home, casts the principal parts among his nearest friends and connections, and rehearses it in downright earnest, with steady nerves and unabated resolution.

Samuel Taylor Coleridge
Lectures on Shakespeare (1818)

Roderigo's description of Othello, as Iago urges him to report the Moor's designs on Desdemona, is the occasion of Coleridge's comment. It is not the blackness of skin but the racial identification with the negro that Coleridge, subject to the social mores of his time, was unable to contemplate. This persistent subjective reaction only serves to highlight the incisive brilliance of Shakespeare's dramatic presentation. The other critical theme, endlessly quoted since, is the question of Iago's motivation, precipitated by Coleridge's commentary on the soliloquy at the end of the first act.

> RODERIGO: What a full fortune does the *thick lips* owe,
> If he can carry't thus.

Roderigo turns off to Othello; and here comes one, if not the only, seeming justification of our blackamoor or negro Othello. Even if we supposed this an uninterrupted tradition of the theatre, and that Shakespeare himself, from want of scenes, and the experience that nothing could be made too marked for the senses of his audience, had practically sanctioned it, - would this prove aught concerning his own intention as a poet for all ages? Can we imagine him so utterly ignorant as to make a barbarous negro plead royal birth, - at a time, too, when negroes were not known except as slaves? - As for Iago's language to Brabantio, it implies merely that Othello was a Moor, that is, black. Though I think the rivalry of Roderigo sufficient to account for his wilful confusion of Moor and Negro, - yet, even if compelled to give this up, I should think it only adapted for the acting of the day, and we should complain of an enormity built on a single word, in direct contradiction to Iago's 'Barbary horse.' Besides, if we could in good earnest believe Shakespeare ignorant of the distinction, still why should we adopt one disagreeable possibility instead of a ten times greater and more pleasing probability? It is a common error to mistake the epithets applied by the *dramatis personae* to each other, as truly descriptive of what the audience ought to see or know. No doubt Desdemona saw Othello's visage in his mind; yet, as we are constituted, and most surely as an English audience was disposed in the beginning of the seventeenth century, it would be something monstrous to conceive this beautiful Venetian girl falling in love with a veritable negro. It would argue a disproportionateness, a want of balance, in Desdemona, which Shakespeare does not appear to have in the least contemplated. . . .

> Go to; farewell! put money enough in your purse!
> [*Exit Roderigo*]
> Thus do I ever make my fool my purse:
> For I mine own gain'd knowledge should profane,
> If I would time expend with such a snipe,
> But for my sport and profit: I hate the Moor . . .

Iago's soliloquy - the motive-hunting of a motiveless malignity - how awful it is! Yea, whilst he is still allowed to bear the divine image, it is too fiendish for his own steady view, - for the lonely gaze of a being next to devil, and only not quite devil, - and yet a character which Shakespeare has attempted and executed, without disgust and without scandal.

A. C. Bradley
Shakespearean Tragedy (1904)

The close-knit structure of Othello, *the emotional excitement aroused by the theme of sexual jealousy, the passivity of Desdemona's love complicated by her husband's colour, and the closeness of the plot to ordinary life, are familar critical points accepted by Bradley. In his approach through psychological realism he is led to a view of Othello as absolute in trust, and of untainted nobility, whose downfall is essentially the result of Iago's villainous intrigue. It follows that Coleridge's description of Iago as embodying 'motiveless malignity' is not acceptable to Bradley, who insists that Iago is an intelligible characterization, motivated by a sense of power and delight in his own skill mingled with ambition and hatred. This view of the dominating role played by Iago against a Romantic paragon was challenged by realists like Stoll who explained Othello in terms of theatrical artifice, and later by interpreters of character psychology who saw an Othello more likely to respond to the suggestion of sexual infidelity from the depths of his own being.*

This character is so noble. Othello's feelings and actions follow so inevitably from it and from the forces brought to bear on it, and his sufferings are so heart-rending, that he stirs, I believe, in most readers a passion of mingled love and pity which they feel for no other hero in Shakespeare, and to which not even Mr. Swinburne can do more than justice. Yet there are some critics and not a few readers who cherish a grudge against him. They do not merely think that in the later stages of his temptation he showed a certain obtuseness, and that, to speak pedantically, he acted with unjustifiable precipitance and violence; no one, I suppose, denies that. But, even when they admit that he was not of a jealous temper, they consider that he *was* 'easily jealous'; they seem to think that it was inexcusable in him to feel any suspicion of his wife at all; and they blame him for never suspecting Iago or asking him for evidence. I refer to this attitude of mind chiefly in order to draw attention to certain points in the story. It comes partly from mere inattention (for Othello did suspect Iago and did ask him for evidence); partly from a misconstruction of the text which makes Othello appear jealous long before he really is so; and partly from failure to realise certain essential facts. I will begin with these.

(1) Othello, we have seen was trustful, and thorough in his trust. He put entire confidence in the honesty of Iago, who had not only been his companion in arms, but, as he believed, had just proved his faithfulness in the matter of the marriage. This confidence was misplaced, and we happen to know it; but it was no sign of stupidity in Othello. For his opinion of Iago was the opinion of practically everyone who knew him: and that opinion was that Iago was before all things 'honest', his very faults being those of excess in honesty. This being so, even if Othello had not been trustful and simple, it would have been quite unnatural in him to be unmoved by the warnings of so honest a friend, warnings offered with extreme reluctance and manifestly from a sense of a friend's duty. *Any* husband would have been troubled by them.

(2) Iago does not bring these warnings to a husband who had lived with a wife for months and years and knew her like his sister or his bosom-friend. Nor is there any ground in Othello's character for supposing that, if he had been such a man, he would have felt and acted as he does in the play. But he was newly married; in the circumstances he cannot have known much of Desdemona before his marriage; and further he was conscious of being under the spell of feeling which can give glory to the truth but can also give it to a dream.

(3) This consciousness in any imaginative man is enough, in such circumstances, to destroy his confidence in his powers of perception. In Othello's case, after a long and most artful preparation, there now comes, to reinforce its effect, the suggestions that he is not an Italian, nor even a European; that he is totally ignorant of the thoughts and the customary morality of Venetian women; that he had himself seen in Desdemona's deception of her father how perfect an actress she could be. As he listens in horror, for a moment at least the past is revealed to him in a new and dreadful light, and the ground seems to

sink under his feet. These suggestions are followed by a tentative but hideous and humiliating insinuation of what his honest and much-experienced friend fears may be the true explanation of Desdemona's rejection of acceptable suitors, and of her strange, and naturally temporary, preference for a black man. Here Iago goes too far. He sees something in Othello's face that frightens him, and he breaks off. Nor does this idea take any hold in Othello's mind. . . .

Now I repeat that *any* man situated as Othello was would have been disturbed by Iago's communications, and I add that many men would have been made wildly jealous. But up to this point, where Iago is dismissed, Othello, I must maintain, does not show jealousy, he feels even horror; but he is not jealous in the proper sense of that word. In his soliloquy (III. iii. 258 ff.) the beginning of this passion may be traced; but it is only after an interval of solitude, when he has time to dwell on the idea presented to him, and especially after statements of fact, not mere general grounds of suspicion, are offered, that the passion lays hold of him. Even then, however, and indeed to the very end, he is quite unlike the essentially jealous man, quite unlike Leontes. No doubt the thought of another man's possessing the woman he loves is intolerable to him; no doubt the sense of insult and the impulse of revenge are at times most violent; and these are the feelings of jealousy proper. But these are not the chief or the deepest source of Othello's suffering. It is the wreck of his faith and his love.
. . .

Up to this point, it appears to me, there is not a syllable to be said against Othello. But the play is a tragedy, and from this point we may abandon the ungrateful and undramatic task of awarding praise and blame. . . .

The Othello of the Fourth Act is Othello in his fall. His fall is never complete, but he is much changed. Towards the close of the Temptation scene he becomes at times most terrible, but his grandeur remains almost undiminished. Even in the following scene (III. iv), where he goes to test Desdemona in the matter of the handkerchief, and receives a fatal confirmation of her guilt, our sympathy with him is hardly touched by any feeling of humiliation. But in the Fourth Act 'Chaos has come.' . . .

But before the end there is again a change. The supposed death of Cassio (V. i) satiates the thirst for vengeance. The Othello who enters the bed-chamber with the words,

> It is the cause, it is the cause, my soul,

is not the man of the Fourth Act. The deed he is bound to do is no murder, but a sacrifice. He is to save Desdemona from herself, not in hate but in honour; in honour, and also in love. His anger has passed; a boundless sorrow has taken its place; and

> this sorrow's heavenly
> It strikes where it doth love.

Even when, at the sight of her apparent obduracy, and at the hearing of words which by a crowning fatality can only reconvince him of her guilt, these feelings give way to others, it is to righteous indignation they give way, not to rage; and, terribly painful as this scene is, there is almost nothing here to diminish the admiration and love which heighten pity. And pity itself vanishes, and love and admiration alone remain, in the majestic dignity and sovereign ascendancy of the close. Chaos has come and gone; and the Othello of the Council-chamber and the quay of Cyprus has returned, or a greater and nobler Othello still. As he speaks those final words in which all the glory and agony of his life – long ago in India and Arabia and Aleppo, and afterwards in Venice, and now in Cyprus – seem to pass before us, like the pictures that flash before the eyes of a drowning man, a triumphant scorn for the fetters of the flesh and the littleness of all the lives that must survive him sweeps our grief away, and when he dies upon a kiss the most painful of all tragedies leaves us for the moment free from pain, and exulting in the power of 'love and man's unconquerable mind.' . . .

Iago stands supreme among Shakespeare's evil characters because the greatest intensity and subtlety of imagination have gone to his making, and because he illustrates in the most perfect combination the two facts concerning evil which seems to have impressed Shakespeare most. The first of these is the fact that perfectly sane people exist in whom fellow-feeling of any kind is so weak that an almost absolute egoism becomes possible to them, and with it those hard vices – such as ingratitude and cruelty – which to Shakespeare were far the worst. The second is that such evil is compatible, and even appears to ally itself easily, with exceptional powers of will and intellect. . . .

In the first place, Iago is not merely negative or evil – far from it. Those very forces that moved him and made his fate – the sense of power, delight in performing a difficult and dangerous action, delight in the exercise of artistic skill – are not at all evil things. We sympathise with one or other of them almost every day of our lives. And, accordingly, although in Iago they are combined with something detestable and so contribute to evil our perception of them is accompanied with sympathy. In the same way, Iago's insight, dexterity, quickness, address, and the like, are in themselves admirable things; the perfect man would possess them. And certainly he would possess also Iago's courage and self-control, and, like Iago, would stand above the impulses of mere feeling, lord of his inner world. All this goes to evil ends in Iago, but in itself it has great worth; and, although in reading, of course, we do not sift it out and regard it separately, it inevitably affects us and mingles admiration with our hatred or horror.

All this, however, might apparently co-exist with absolute egoism and total want of humanity. But in the second place, it is not true that in Iago this egoism and this want are absolute, and that in this sense he is a thing of mere evil. They are frightful, but if they were absolute Iago would be a monster, not a man. The fact is, he *tries* to make them absolute and cannot succeed; and the traces of conscience, shame and humanity, though faint, are discernible. If his egoism were absolute he would be perfectly indifferent to the opinion of others; and he clearly is not so. His very irritation at goodness, again, is a sign that his faith in his creed is not entirely firm; and it is not entirely firm because he himself has a perception, however dim, of the goodness of goodness. . . .

There remains, thirdly, the idea that Iago is a man of supreme intellect who is at the same time supremely wicked. That he is supremely wicked nobody will doubt; and I have claimed for him nothing that will interfere with his right to that title. But to say that his intellectual power is supreme is to make a great mistake. Within certain limits he has indeed extraordinary penetration, quickness, inventiveness, adaptiveness; but the limits are defined with the hardest of lines, and they are narrow limits. It would scarcely be unjust to call him simply astonishingly clever, or simply a consummate master of intrigue. But compare him with one who may perhaps be roughly called a bad man of supreme intellectual power, Napoleon, and you see how small and negative Iago's mind is, incapable of Napoleon's military achievements, and much more incapable of his political constructions. Or, to keep within the Shakespearean world, compare him with Hamlet, and you perceive how miserably close is his intellectual horizon; that such a thing as a thought beyond the reaches of his soul has ever come near him; that he is prosaic through and through, deaf and blind to all but a tiny fragment of the meaning of things. Is it not quite absurd, then, to call him a man of supreme intellect?

And observe, lastly, that his failure in perception is closely connected with his badness. He was destroyed by the power that he attacked, the power of love; and he was destroyed by it because he could not understand it; and he could not understand it because it was not in him. Iago never meant his plot to be so dangerous to himself. He knew that jealousy is painful, but the jealousy of a love like Othello's he could not imagine, and he found himself involved in murders which were no part of his original design. That difficulty he surmounted, and his changed plot still seemed to prosper. Roderigo and Cassio and Desdemona once dead, all will be well. He will avow that he told Othello of the adultery, and persist that he told the truth, and Cassio will deny it in vain. And then, in a moment, his plot is shattered by a blow from a quarter where he never dreamt of danger. He knows his wife, he thinks. She is not over-scrupulous, she will do anything to please him, and she has learnt obedience. But one thing in her he does not know – that she *loves* her mistress and would face a hundred deaths sooner than see her fair fame darkened. There is genuine astonishment in his outburst 'What! Are you mad?' as it dawns upon him that she means to speak the truth about the handkerchief. But he might well have applied to himself the words she flings at Othello,

> O gull! O dolt!
> As ignorant as dirt!

The foulness of his own soul made him so ignorant that he built into the marvellous structure of his plot a piece of crass stupidity.

To the thinking mind the divorce of unusual intellect from goodness is a thing to startle; and Shakespeare clearly felt it so. The combination of unusual intellect with extreme evil is more than startling, it is frightful. It is rare, but it exists; and Shakespeare represented it in Iago. But the alliance of evil like Iago's with *supreme* intellect is an impossible fiction; and Shakespeare's fictions were truth.

Elmer Edgar Stoll
Art and Artifice in Shakespeare (1933)

The contrast between Othello and Iago is accepted by Stoll, but the tragic change in Othello he explains as dramatic contrivance not psychological formula. Shakespeare's preoccupation, for Stoll, is not with life but with an illusion of life, and there are therefore different apprehensions of Othello and Iago. Preservation of the 'illusion of delusion' explains Iago's success in dissimulation, and the apparent denial of Othello's jealousy. What in real life might appear as psychological inconsistency is explained by Stoll as deliberate artifice for dramatic purposes. He castigates the spirit of literalism in criticism, arguing for acceptance of the dramatic effectiveness of the protagonists, not an examination of their suitability as clinical case-histories. Bradley's picture of a noble Othello trapped by the villainous intellect of Iago and Stoll's alternative version of 'realism' and theatrical contrivance were both to be challenged, notably by F. R. Leavis (in 'Diabolic Intellect and the Noble Hero' included in The Common Pursuit) *who regarded Iago as 'subordinate and merely ancillary' and Othello as carrying the seeds of his own destruction. Nevertheless, Leavis himself was led to conclude that Othello would probably remain for many 'the entirely noble hero', and he exonerates Shakespeare from censure, even though he found the brilliance and poignancy of the play still left it below the greatest of the works. Stoll's stimulating critical contribution certainly led to a modification of Bradley, and laid the foundation for a critical debate which continues.*

The trouble is, that the critics have been taking fiction for fact; that they will have no disbelief on the part of the spectator at the outset, but only belief, or if disbelief suspended, then not 'for the moment' but for all time; that they turn the impossibilities into possibilities, and the poetry into prose; that their ears are caught by the weaker accents, not the stronger. They have been laboriously quibbling and hair-splitting to keep even with him who lightly manœuvred and manipulated. They have been twisting and stretching their psychology to justify him as he frankly, but authoritatively, adopted an initial postulate for a great dramatic effect. And what effect is that? It is one of accumulation and compression, of simplification and concentration; to which all art, and especially drama, tends. It is a more startling and passionate contrast, an accelerated movement, a more unmingled sympathy with both hero and heroine. I do not mean the contrast between Othello innocent and noble and Iago cunning and wicked, though it of course is there; but that in the hero himself, between his love, which is native to him, and a hatred that has not (as ordinarily) been slowly and grossly bred out of it, but has sprung up full-grown at its side. There is, as there should be, a remarkable identity of tone to the hero's voice when uttering either passion; but nowhere else in drama is there a contrast so poignant as this between them, and also between what he feels and what he does, and between what he says and does since the temptation, on the one hand, and before it and after the clearing up at the end, on the other. Both before and after, Othello is probably the most noble and engaging of all the heroes of drama or of epic; and how could the effect of the intervening change have been so striking, so tragic and heart-rending, if 'easily' – naturally – he had become so jealous?

It is a mechanical device, to be sure, this intrusion of the villain; but there is something of the mechanical in most art, once we get to the bottom of it. It is in a fugue and in a symphony, and of much the same sort in a great fugue or symphony and a mediocre. This difference of quality lies not in the contrivance itself but in the use of it, in what is thereby contrived. And that we are not going astray in finding this particular mechanism here is evident not only from its fitness to the plain meaning of the text and the nature of the character and the situation, but also from its superiority in these regards to the psychological formula offered, with its claptrap and legerdemain. The present interpretation does not at the point in question represent the image of life, but it does not pretend to do so; and is itself, I hope, true to the play and other plays, to the nature of the theatre and the capacity of the audience. The psychological interpretation with a trustfulness which distrusts, and belief which directly leads to disbelief (and of the wrong person in either case) – all in a healthy, discerning, and noble mind, not diseased or perverted – is true neither to the facts of the play nor, for all its pretensions, to those of life as we know it. What does it profit us to make Shakespeare out a psychological oracle, if such be his doctrine? . . .

For many elements go to the making of a tragedy, as of any great work of art; and many and diverse considerations of which he is not fully conscious prompt the artist. Those, however, which we have been noticing, and are yet to notice, are entirely artistic ones, whereby he *may* have been prompted; not psychological, philosophical, or present-day notions, which were not within his or his spectators' purview. They have to do with the play as a whole, not some passage or two within it; with the actual expression, not what the dramatist is supposed to be dimly thinking of, or we have started thinking of ourselves. Only as an artist, not as a philosopher or psychologist, did he or any other dramatist ever build better than he knew; and even as such, save as he was but following tradition, he, on reflection, knew well enough (that is, could see that he was right), though possibly he was not critical - analytical - enough to explain it. And what Shakespeare is here preoccupied with, as we have in part seen, is not primarily the image of life but an illusion, and, as its consequence, a greater emotional effect than the mere image of life can give. In a great work of art everything is reciprocal; and though our description of the means whereby the illusion is here secured is as yet incomplete, we have already seen the emotional force, set free by the initial premise, itself contributing to the illusion. But this could not take place by warrant of the premise alone. That action must needs be supported by others, or rather, it must be extended and confirmed. If the hero's prestige is to be safeguarded, and our sympathy irrevocably engaged, the matter of Othello's mind being open and undefended but Iago's impenetrable, involves that of the villain's seeming so, and the hero's *not* seeming so, to all the other characters, and that of Iago's reputation for superlative wisdom into the bargain . . . .

On the head of Iago's intellectual gifts the critics have been divided - some thinking them supreme, others limited. Some dwell on his uniform success; others, noting the prodigious risks he ran and his final failure, call it luck; both parties alike treating him as if an authenticated case, and the play as if a chapter of his 'life-story.' Out in the world any man whose reputation for honesty and wisdom was so complete and spotless should for this very reason, have been a little questionable, like that of the bank-cashier–Sunday-school-superintendents in small undefended towns a generation ago. But the mere illusion, on the stage, has by the dramatist been achieved as skilfully in regard to wisdom as to honesty: every one there explicitly or implicitly acknowledges it. And in the theatre he achieves the corresponding effect, of knavish craftiness, not only by Iago's success (whether in his own playing or in pulling the strings for the puppets), but also (which is still more important) by his manifest superiority in thought and speech. There is witch-craft, though not like the poet's own, in his lips. His art is the black, and the ritual, of woven paces and waving hands, is in his lines.

No one like Shakespeare in *Othello* has created and preserved the illusion of delusion; and that is the reason he has taken such pains to deny his hero the jealous nature. Thereby he derives from the initial fiction its full dramatic advantage and virtue: by giving the Moor the 'predisposition', making the character more psychological and the situation more probable, he would be throwing much of this away. Some of the critics who find the improbability, not in the mere change within the hero, but in the fact that Desdemona has had no time or opportunity to be unfaithful, have shown how easily it could have been provided. She and Emilia might have made the voyage with Cassio instead of Iago. But Shakespeare, who, of course, and rightly, does not raise the question, will no more give Othello evidence or justification for suspicion than the predisposition itself. By the impenetrableness of Iago's mask he can have a hero who has nothing in him of the simpleton or gull; by the want of a suspicious nature he can have a hero who is wholly noble and lovable. Thus he achieves a greater complication – a generous nature in a jealous rage. . . .

Why does not Shakespeare content himself with the simple contrast of Othello serene and noble at the beginning and (though broken) at the end, and Othello jealous and furious in between? By the Elizabethan audience the words about jealousy of Desdemona and Emilia, Lodovico and Iago, and the Moor himself, were doubtless not needed (sorely as they are by the critics) for the guidance of their minds, but only for their emotions; and they are designed mainly to direct attention to the tragic change. And why from the outset does the dramatist make nearly every character but the villain unreservedly love and admire the hero as well as the heroine, and these speak and act in such a way that the audience does too? Instead of bridging the gap, he widens it, and points to it, careful still, not for the psychology, but the immediate effect; and the wonder and dismay, felt on every hand, is not only a note of reality but a stroke of emphasis, both of which make the contrast count. Desdemona's remark about the handkerchief before Othello's entry, that, save for the fact that he is 'made of no such baseness as jealous creatures are, it were enough to put him to ill thinking'; Emilia's question upon his exit, 'Is not this man jealous?' and Desdemona's bewildered reply; Lodovico's 'Is this the noble Moor whom our full Senate call all in all sufficient?', Iago's headshake in answer, and Othello's own 'not easily jealous' at the close – all these throw the intervening situation, which intrinsically deserves it, into high relief. And though by Shakespeare's art he is (as we have seen and are yet to see) in a manner still kept before us, we painfully miss the hero, and vividly recall him (while Lodovico continues), as he was:

> Is this the nature
> Whom passion could not shake? whose solid virtue
> The shot of accident nor dart of chance
> Could neither graze nor pierce?

The irony is that of fact, not of fact and opinion: these minor characters, in noting the change, are as right as a Greek chorus. The villain, as often in Elizabethan tragedy, takes the place of the ancient Fate: and these repeated personal reactions bring the irony home. This villain, by all this contriving of the poet's, bears in this instance, like the ancient Fate or intruding god, the burden of responsibility; and our sympathy with a hero made of no such baseness is almost without alloy. . . .

The trouble with Shakespeare criticism, as we have already noticed, is that it has been prompted and guided by the spirit of literalism. The play has been thought to be a psychological document, not primarily a play, a structure, both interdependent and independent, the parts mutually, and sufficiently, supporting and explaining each other; and the characters have been taken for the separable copies of reality. At bottom the mistake is the same as that of the actors, who, as Heine said, were in his day concerned only for the characterization, 'not at all for the poetry and still less for the art.' But if one character be so interpreted the others must be; if Othello is a study in psychology and tragic error, then not only he but nearly everybody else in the play must be stupid, and Emilia must be either stupid or disloyal, or else, indeed, a prey to an abrupt and disenchanting intrusion of the plot. And then her conduct is not probable; whereas by our interpretation it is, that is (in Croce's sense of the word) *coherent*, in harmony with the whole. How much finer in the poet, and more satisfying to the imagination, that the characters, one and all, should thus be deftly transported into another world, and made subject to the high and all-prevailing purpose of a tragic illusion; and that the play should be, not a transcript of fact, but, as Pater says, of the poet's sense of fact – not a cluster of studies embedded in a story, but a new creation and an individual, unbroken whole! And in so saying we are not speaking in riddles or trafficking in mysteries, but heeding the highest critical wisdom of the ages.

KING LEAR (1605-1606)

It has been claimed that in the twentieth century *King Lear* has replaced *Hamlet* as the Shakespearean tragedy held in the highest esteem. The play once notoriously regarded as un-actable is now considered to provide a challenging opportunity for Shakespearean actors to achieve the ultimate theatrical success. For long the literary bias in criticism regarded *King Lear* as something of a retrogression, a return to the loose episodic structure of the chronicle history play coming so soon after the close-knit dramatic form of *Othello*. The change above all illustrates that Shakespeare does not sink into any conforming mould in his approach to tragedy. Even modern criticism has paid more attention to *King Lear* as a poetic *tour de force* than as a compelling dramatic experience. Although the play's suitability for the theatre is now accepted, the difficulty of representing its tragic impact fully and successfully is also recognized. On the one hand the tragedy has been interpreted as a ruthless and pessimistic evocation of a pagan world; on the other it has been seen as providing a Christian perspective on paganism, with social, political, and ethical implications. The power and range of the poetry, the metaphysical sweep which explores the clash between a divinely controlled nature and an anarchic survival struggle, have long been acclaimed. Increasingly the dramatic power of the poetry has been held as more than redeeming the apparent structural weakness of the play.

Samuel Johnson
The Plays of Shakespeare (1765)

Romantic reservations about the staging of King Lear *are not shared by Dr Johnson, although with the important proviso that he accepts Nahum Tate's alterations to the play which long held the stage. The unhappiness of the ending disappears in Tate's version of 1681, with Cordelia married, Lear restored, and the Fool dropped from the play altogether. Johnson gave critical support, and loses no opportunity to stress the moral justice which ensues. The improbabilities of the tragedy Johnson excuses on historical grounds, but the violation of his sense of classical decorum prompts him to reject the blinding of Gloucester, a critical theme which would continue.*

The tragedy of Lear is deservedly celebrated among the dramas of Shakespeare. There is perhaps no play which keeps the attention so strongly fixed; which so much agitates our passions and interests our curiosity. The artful involutions of distinct interests, the striking opposition of contrary characters, the sudden changes of fortune, and the quick succession of events, fill the mind with a perpetual tumult of indignation, pity, and hope. There is no scene which does not contribute to the aggravation of the distress or conduct of the action, and scarce a line which does not conduce to the progress of the scene. So powerful is the current of the poet's imagination, that the mind, which once ventures within it, is hurried irresistibly along.

On the seeming improbability of Lear's conduct it may be observed, that he is represented according to histories at that time vulgarly received as true. And perhaps if we turn our thoughts upon the barbarity and ignorance of the age to which this story is referred, it will appear not so unlikely as while we estimate Lear's manners by our own. Such preference of one daughter to another, or resignation of dominion on such conditions, would be yet credible, if told of a petty prince of Guinea or Madagascar. Shakespeare, indeed, by the mention of his earls and dukes, has given us the idea of times more civilised, and of life regulated by softer manners; and the truth is, that though he so nicely discriminates, and so minutely describes the characters of men, he commonly neglects and confounds the characters of ages, by mingling customs ancient and modern, English and foreign.

My learned friend Mr. Warton, who has in the *Adventurer* very minutely criticised this play, remarks, that the instances of cruelty are too savage and shocking, and that the intervention of Edmund destroys the simplicity of the story. These objections may, I think, be answered by repeating, that the cruelty of the daughters is an historical fact, to which the poet has added little, having only drawn it into a series by dialogue and action. But I am not able to apologise with equal plausibility for the extrusion of Gloucester's eyes, which seems an act too horrid to be endured in dramatick exhibition, and such as must always compel the mind to relieve its distress by incredulity. Yet let it be remembered that our author well knew what would please the audience for which he wrote.

The injury done by Edmund to the simplicity of the action is abundantly recompensed by the addition of variety, by the art with which he is made to co-operate with the chief design, and the opportunity which he gives the poet of combining perfidy with perfidy, and connecting the wicked son with the wicked daughters, to impress this important moral, that villainy is never at a stop, that crimes lead to crimes, and at last terminate in ruin.

But though this moral be incidentally enforced, Shakespeare has suffered the virtue of Cordelia to perish in a just cause, contrary to the natural ideas of justice, to the hope of the reader, and, what is yet more strange, to the faith of chronicles. Yet this conduct is justified by the Spectator [Joseph Addison in *Spectator*, no. 40], who blames Tate for giving Cordelia success and happiness in his alteration, and declares, that, in his opinion, 'the tragedy has lost half its beauty.' Dennis has remarked, whether justly or not, that, to secure the favourable reception of *Cato*, 'the town was poisoned with much false and abominable criticism,' and that endeavours had been used to discredit and decry poetical justice. A play in which the wicked prosper, and the virtuous miscarry, may doubtless be good, because it is a just representation of the common events of human life: but since all reasonable beings naturally love justice, I cannot easily be persuaded, that the observation of justice makes a play worse; or, that if other excellencies are equal, the audience will not always rise better pleased from the final triumph of persecuted virtue.

In the present case the public has decided. Cordelia, from the time of Tate, has always retired with victory and felicity. And, if my sensations could add any thing to the general suffrage, I might relate, that I was many years ago so shocked by Cordelia's death, that I know not whether I ever endured to read again the last scenes of the play till I undertook to revise them as an editor.

Charles Lamb
On the Tragedies of Shakespeare (1811)

This scornful dismissal of attempts to present King Lear *on the stage in fact contains significant recognition of those universal aspects of the poetry of the tragedy which have been praised by modern critics. For Lamb no acting could achieve this kind of insight, and his condemnation of Tate's alterations to the play are at one with his dissatisfaction with contemporary theatrical presentation. In spirit, with his plea for an imaginative interpretation, Lamb is closer to modern approaches to the drama than he is often given credit for.*

To see Lear acted, – to see an old man tottering about the stage with a walking-stick, turned out of doors by his daughters in a rainy night, has nothing in it but what is painful and disgusting. We want to take him into shelter and relieve him. That is all the feeling which the acting of Lear ever produced in me. But the Lear of Shakespeare cannot be acted. The contemptible machinery by which they mimic the storm which he goes out in, is not more inadequate to represent the horrors of the real elements, than any actor can be to represent Lear: they might more easily propose to personate the Satan of Milton upon a stage, or one of Michael Angelo's terrible figures. The greatness of Lear is not in corporal dimension, but in intellectual: the explosions of his passion are terrible as a volcano: they are storms turning up and disclosing to the bottom that sea, his mind, with all its vast riches. It is his mind which is laid bare. This case of flesh and blood seems too insignificant to be thought on: even as he himself neglects it. On the stage we see nothing but corporal infirmities and weakness, the impotence of rage; while we read it, we see not Lear, but we are Lear, – we are in his mind, we are sustained by a grandeur which baffles the malice of daughters and storms; in the aberrations of his reason, we discover a mighty irregular power of reasoning, immethodized from the ordinary purposes of life, but exerting its powers, as the wind blows where it listeth, at will upon the corruptions and abuses of mankind. What have looks, or tones, to do with that sublime identification of his age with that of the *heavens themselves*, when in his reproaches to them for conniving at the injustice of his children, he reminds them that 'they themselves are old.' What gesture shall we appropriate to this? What has the voice or the eye to do with such things? But the play is beyond all art, as the tamperings with it shew: it is too hard and stony; it must have love-scenes, and a happy ending. It is not enough that Cordelia is a daughter, she must shine as a lover too. Tate has put his hook in the nostrils of this Leviathan, for Garrick and his followers, the showmen of the scene, to draw the mighty beast about more easily. A happy ending! – as if the living martyrdom that Lear had gone through, – the flaying of his feelings alive, did not make a fair dismissal from the stage of life the only decorous thing for him. If he is to live and be happy after, if he could sustain this world's burden after, why all this pudder and preparation, – why torment us with all this unnecessary sympathy? As if the childish pleasure of getting his gilt robes and sceptre again could tempt him to act over again his misused station, – as if at his years, and with his experience, any thing was left but to die.

William Hazlitt
'Characters of Shakespeare's Plays' (1817)

King Lear *is rated as the best of Shakespeare's plays by Hazlitt, and he makes apt comparisons with* Othello *in his assessment of the central characterization. Like Coleridge, and many critics to follow, he appreciates the importance of the Fool, and places him in the dramatic structure of the play. For Hazlitt Shakespeare's firm control of the tragic theme requires no adherence to rules, but is exemplified in the ironic reflection of Edgar's assumed in Lear's real madness as the action unfolds.*

We wish we could pass this play over, and say nothing about it. All that we can say must fall far short of the subject; or even of what we ourselves conceive of it. To attempt to give a description of the play itself or of its effect upon the mind, is mere impertinence: yet we must say something. It is then the best of all Shakespeare's plays, for it is the one in which he was the most in earnest. He was here fairly caught in the web of his own imagination. The passion which he has taken as his subject is that which strikes its roots deepest into the human heart; of which the bond is the hardest to be unloosed; and the cancelling and tearing to pieces of which gives the greatest revulsion to the frame. This depth of nature, this force of passion, this tug of war of the elements of our being, this firm faith in filial piety, and the giddy anarchy and whirling tumult of the thoughts at finding this prop failing it, the contrast between the fixed, immoveable basis of natural affection, and the rapid, irregular starts of imagination, suddenly wrenched from all its accustomed holds and resting-places in the soul, this is what Shakespeare has given, and what nobody else but he could give. So we believe. – The mind of Lear, staggering between the weight of attachment and the hurried movements of passion, is like a tall ship driven about by the winds, buffeted by the furious waves, but that still rides above the storm, having its anchor fixed in the bottom of the sea; or it is like the sharp rock circled by the eddying whirlpool that foams and beats against it or like the solid promontory pushed from its basis by the force of an earthquake. . ..

We have seen in *Othello*, how the unsuspecting frankness and impetuous passions of the Moor are played upon and exasperated by the artful dexterity of Iago. In the present play, that which aggravates the sense of sympathy in the reader, and of uncontrollable anguish in the swollen heart of Lear, is the petrifying indifference, the cold, calculating, obdurate selfishness of his daughters. His keen passions seem whetted on their stony hearts. The contrast would be too painful, the shock too great, but for the intervention of the Fool, whose well-timed levity comes in to break the continuity of feeling when it can no longer be borne, and to bring into play again the fibres of the heart just as they are growing rigid from over-strained excitement. The imagination is glad to take refuge in the half-comic, half-serious comments of the Fool, just as the mind under the extreme anguish of a surgical operation vents itself in sallies of wit. The character was also a grotesque ornament of the barbarous times, in which alone the tragic groundwork of the story could be laid. In another point of view it is indispensable, inasmuch as while it is a diversion to the too great intensity of our disgust, it carries the pathos to the highest pitch of which it is capable, by showing the pitiable weakness of the old king's conduct and its irretrievable consequences in the most familar point of view. Lear may well 'beat at the gate which let his folly in,' after, as the Fool says, 'he has made his daughters his mothers.' The character is dropped in the third act to make room for the entrance of Edgar as Mad Tom, which well accords with the increasing bustle and wildness of the incidents; and nothing can be more complete than the distinction between Lear's real and Edgar's assumed madness, while the resemblance in the cause of their distresses, from the severing of the nearest ties of natural affection, keeps up a unity of interest. Shakespeare's mastery over his subject, if it was not art, was owing to a knowledge of the connecting links of the passions, and their effect upon the mind, still more wonderful than any systematic adherence to rules, and that anticipated and outdid all the efforts of the most refined art, not inspired and rendered instinctive by genius.

Samuel Taylor Coleridge
Lectures on Shakespeare (1818)

Coleridge thinks King Lear *is founded on improbabilities but nevertheless praises Shakespeare's judgment in developing the theme of filial ingratitude. Impatience with Lear's early conduct is a common enough complaint, but Coleridge praises the skill with which the other characters are developed to serve the tragic theme, particularly the Fool. Like Johnson, Coleridge deplores that affront to classical decorum, the blinding of Gloucester. Later criticism was to be less concerned with improbabilities and characterization, and more with the power of the language.*

Of all Shakespeare's plays *Macbeth* is the most rapid, *Hamlet* the slowest, in movement. *Lear* combines length with rapidity, – like the hurricane and the whirlpool, absorbing while it advances. It begins as a stormy day in summer, with brightness; but that brightness is lurid, and anticipates the tempest.

It was not without forethought, nor is it without its due significance, that the division of Lear's kingdom is in the first six lines of the play stated as a thing already determined in all its particulars, previously to the trial of professions, as the relative rewards of which the daughters were to be made to consider their several portions. The strange, yet by no means unnatural, mixture of selfishness, sensibility, and habit of feeling derived from, and fostered by, the particular rank and usages of the individual; – the intense desire of being intensely beloved, – selfish, and yet characteristic of the selfishness of a loving and kindly nature alone; – the self-supporting leaning for all pleasure on another's breast; – the craving after sympathy with a prodigal disinterestedness, frustrated by its own ostentation, and the mode and nature of its claims; – the anxiety, the distrust, the jealousy, which more or less accompany all selfish affections, and are amongst the surest contradistinctions of mere fondness from true love, and which originate Lear's eager wish to enjoy his daughter's violent professions, whilst the inveterate habits of sovereignty convert the wish into claim and positive right, and an incompliance with it into crime and treason; – these facts, these passions, these moral verities, on which the whole tragedy is founded, are all prepared for, and will to the retrospect be found implied, in these first four or five lines of the play. They let us know that the trial is but a trick; and that the grossness of the old king's rage is in part the natural result of a silly trick suddenly and most unexpectedly baffled and disappointed.

It may here be worthy of notice, that Lear is the only serious performance of Shakespeare, the interest and situations of which are derived from the assumption of a gross improbability; whereas Beaumont and Fletcher's tragedies are, almost all of them, founded on some out of the way accident or exception to the general experience of mankind. But observe the matchless judgment of our Shakespeare. First, improbable as the conduct of Lear is in the first scene, yet it was an old story rooted in the popular faith, – a thing taken for granted already, and consequently without any of the effects of improbability. Secondly, it is merely the canvass for the characters and passions, – a mere occasion for, – and not, in the manner of Beaumont and Fletcher, perpetually recurring as the cause, and *sine qua non* of, – the incidents and emotions. Let the first scene of this play have been lost,

126

and let it only be understood that a fond father had been duped by hypocritical professions of love and duty on the part of two daughters to disinherit the third, previously, and deservedly, more dear to him; – and all the rest of the tragedy would retain its interest undiminished, and be perfectly intelligible. The accidental is nowhere the groundwork of the passions, but that which is catholic, which in all ages has been, and ever will be, close and native to the heart of man, – parental anguish from filial ingratitude, the genuineness of worth, though confined in bluntness, and the execrable vileness of a smooth iniquity. . . .

The Fool is no comic buffoon to make the groundlings laugh, – no forced condescension of Shakespeare's genius to the taste of his audience. Accordingly the poet prepares for his introduction, which he never does with any of his common clowns and fools, by bringing him into living connection with the pathos of the play. He is as wonderful a creation as Caliban; – his wild babblings, and inspired idiocy, articulate and gauge the horrors of the scene.

A. C. Bradley
Shakespearean Tragedy (1904)

Lamb's complete dismissal of King Lear *from the theatre is qualified by Bradley, who accepts the theatrical effectiveness of some of the scenes, but agrees that important attributes of its peculiar greatness are beyond theatrical presentation. What have often been regarded as the more obvious theatrical absurdities of the opening scene and Gloucester's supposed leap from the cliff top at Dover are not dramatic blemishes for Bradley, but he does agree with Coleridge and Johnson in rejecting the spectacle of the blinding of Gloucester. Admitting to a heresy, Bradley even acknowledges that an ending with Lear and Cordelia saved could be justified, prompting no lack of comment from later critics. The allegation of structural weakness is at the core of Bradley's criticism of the tragedy, the ill-matched 'double action', multiplicity of character, and vastness of scope beyond the theatre's resources. Many have agreed with Bradley that Shakespeare seemed less concerned with fitness for the stage in* King Lear, *but for all that the tragedy is his greatest achievement, if not his best play. Significantly, Bradley agrees that the approach through psychological realism is not appropriate in this play, although he joins others in regarding the Fool as one of Shakespeare's greatest triumphs. However unsatisfactory he finds its characterization, and however defective he finds the structure, Bradley has no doubt that in* King Lear *Shakespeare has carried the pity and terror of tragedy to its utmost limits, placing the work at the highest level of creative art.*

The stage is the test of strictly dramatic quality, and *King Lear* is too huge for the stage. Of course, I am not denying that it is a great stage-play. It has scenes immensely effective in the theatre; three of them – the two between Lear and Goneril and between Lear, Goneril and Regan, and the ineffably beautiful scene in the Fourth Act between Lear and Cordelia – lose in the theatre very little of the spell they have for the imagination; and the gradual interweaving of the two plots is almost as masterly as in *Much Ado*. But (not to speak of defects due to mere carelessness) that which makes the *peculiar* greatness of *King Lear*, – the immense scope of the work; the mass and variety of intense experience which it contains; the interpenetration of sublime imagination, piercing pathos, and humour almost as moving as the pathos; the vastness of the convulsion both of nature and of human passion; the vagueness of the scene where the action takes place, and the movement of the figures which cross this scene; the strange atmosphere, cold and dark, which strikes on us as we enter this scene, enfolding these figures and magnifying their dim outlines like a winter mist; the half-realised suggestions of vast universal powers working in the world of individual fates and passions, – all this interferes with dramatic clearness even when the play is read, and in the theatre not only refuses to reveal itself fully through the senses but seems to be almost in contradiction with their reports. This is not so with the other great tragedies. No doubt, as Lamb declared, theatrical representation gives only a part of what we imagine when we read them; but there is no *conflict* between the representation and the imagination, because these tragedies are, in essentials, perfectly dramatic. But *King Lear*, as a whole, is imperfectly dramatic, and there is something in its very essence which is at war with the senses, and demands a purely imaginative realisation. It is therefore Shakespeare's greatest work, but it is not what Hazlitt called it, the best of his plays; and its comparative unpopularity is due, not merely to the extreme painfulness of the catastrophe, but in part to its dramatic defects, and in part to a failure in many readers to catch the peculiar effects to which I have referred, – a failure which is natural because the appeal is made not so much to dramatic perception as to a rarer and more strictly poetic kind of imagination. For this reason, too, even the best attempts at exposition of *King Lear* are disappointing; they remind us of attempts to reduce to prose the impalpable spirit of the *Tempest*. . . .

A dramatic mistake in regard to the catastrophe, even supposing it to exist, would not seriously affect the whole play. The principal structural weakness of *King Lear* lies elsewhere. It is felt to some extent in the earlier Acts, but still more (as from our study of Shakespeare's technique we have learnt to expect) in the Fourth and the first part of the Fifth. And it arises chiefly from the double action, which is a peculiarity of *King Lear* among the tragedies. By the side of Lear, his daughters, Kent, and the Fool, who are the principal figures in the main plot, stand Gloster and his two sons, the chief persons of the secondary plot. Now by means of this double action Shakespeare secured certain results highly advantageous even from the strictly dramatic point of view, and easy to perceive. But the disadvantages were dramatically greater. The number of essential characters is so large, their actions and movements are so complicated, and events towards the close crowd on one another so thickly, that the reader's attention, rapidly transferred from one centre of interest to another, is overstrained. He becomes, if not intellectually confused, at least emotionally fatigued. The battle, on which everything turns, scarcely affects him. The deaths of Edmund, Goneril, Regan and Gloster seem 'but trifles here'; and anything short of the incomparable pathos of the close would leave him cold. There is something almost ludicrous in the insignificance of this battle, when it is compared with the corresponding battles in *Julius Caesar* and *Macbeth*; and though there may have been further reasons for its insignificance, the main one is simply that there was no room to give it its due effect among such a host of competing interests.

A comparison of the last two Acts of *Othello* with the last two Acts of *King Lear* would show how unfavourable to dramatic clearness is a multiplicity of figures. But that this multiplicity is not in itself a fatal obstacle is evident from the last two Acts of *Hamlet*, and especially from the final scene. This is in all respects one of Shakespeare's triumphs, yet the stage is crowded with characters. Only they are not *leading* characters. The plot is single; Hamlet and the King are 'mighty opposites'; and Ophelia, the only other person in whom we are obliged to take a vivid interest, has already disappeared. It is therefore natural and right that the deaths of Laertes and the Queen should affect us comparatively little. But in *King Lear*, because the plot is double, we have present in the last scene no less than five persons who are technically of the first importance – Lear, his three daughters and Edmund; not to speak of Kent and Edgar, of whom the latter at any rate is technically quite as important as Laertes. And again, owing to the pressure of persons and events, and owing to the concentration of our anxiety on Lear and Cordelia the combat of Edgar and Edmund, which occupies so considerable a space, fails to excite a tithe of the interest of the fencing match in *Hamlet*. The truth is that all through these Acts Shakespeare has too vast a material to use with complete dramatic effectiveness, however essential this very vastness was for effects of another kind.

Added to these defects there are others, which suggest that in *King Lear* Shakespeare was less concerned than usual with dramatic fitness; improbabilities, inconsistencies, sayings and doings which suggest questions only to be answered by conjecture. The improbabilities in *King Lear* surely far surpass those of the other great tragedies in number and in grossness. And they are particularly noticeable in the secondary plot. . . .

How is it, now that this defective drama so overpowers us that we are either unconscious of its blemishes or regard them as almost irrelevant? As soon as we turn to this question we recognise, not merely that *King Lear* possesses purely dramatic qualities which far outweigh its defects, but that its greatness consists partly in imaginative effects of a wider kind. And, looking for the sources of these effects, we find among them some of those very things which appeared to us dramatically faulty or injurious. Thus, to take at once two of the simplest examples of this, that very vagueness in the sense of locality which we have just considered, and again that excess in the bulk of the material and the number of figures, events and movements, while they interfere with the clearness of vision, have at the same time a positive value for imagination. They give the feeling of vastness, the feeling not of a scene or particular place, but of a world; or, to speak more accurately, of a particular place which is also a world. This world is dim to us, partly from its immensity, and partly because it is filled with gloom; and in the gloom shapes approach and recede, whose half-seen faces and motions touch us with dread, horror, or the most painful pity, – sympathies and antipathies which we seem to be feeling not only for them but for the whole race. This world, we are told is called Britain; but we should no more look for it in an atlas than for the place called Caucasus where Prometheus was chained by Strength and Force and comforted by the daughters of Ocean. . . ..

Hence too, as well as from other sources, comes that feeling which haunts us in *King Lear*, as though we were witnessing something universal, – a conflict not so much of particular persons as of powers of good and evil in the world. And the treatment of many of the characters confirms this feeling. Considered simply as psychological studies few of them, surely, are of the highest interest. Fine and subtle touches could not be absent from a work of Shakespeare's maturity; but, with the possible exception of Lear himself, no one of the characters strikes us as psychologically a *wonderful* creation, like Hamlet or Iago or even Macbeth; one or two seem even to be somewhat faint and thin. And what is more significant, it is not quite natural to us to regard them from this point of view at all.

G. Wilson Knight
The Wheel of Fire (1930)

The strongest answer to Bradley and Lamb regarding the staging of King Lear *came from an actor and producer. H. Granville Barker's* Prefaces to Shakespeare *included the case for the production of even a difficult play like* King Lear, *providing attempts at 'realism' were avoided and the poetry fully utilized. With even Bradley modifying the psychological approach, and staging accepted as an effective possibility, criticism turned to grounds more appropriate for what many regarded as Shakespeare's most profound tragedy. The play's poetic intensity - what Keats referred to as 'the fierce dispute / Betwixt damnation and impassion'd clay' ('On Sitting Down to Read* King Lear *Once Again') - provided the critical focus. No ordinary character analysis is satisfactory for* King Lear, *and Wilson Knight refers to the atmosphere and visionary plane to which the dramatic persons are 'strongly tuned'. The philosophic range of the play, the visionary power straining at the frontiers of drama, the mental atmosphere, are characteristics which henceforth capture critical attention.*

King Lear gives one the impression of life's abundance magnificently compressed into one play.

No Shakespearian play shows so wide a range of sympathetic

creation: we seem to be confronted, not with certain men and women only, but with mankind. It is strange to find that we have been watching little more than a dozen people. *King Lear* is a tragic vision of humanity, in its complexity, its interplay of purpose, its travailing evolution. The play is a microcosm of the human race – strange as that word 'microcosm' sounds for the vastness, the width and depth, the vague vistas which this play reveals. Just as skilful grouping on the stage deceives the eye, causing six men to suggest an army, grouping which points the eye from the stage toward the unactualized spaces beyond which imagination accepts in its acceptance of the stage itself, so the technique here – the vagueness of locality, and of time, the inconsistencies and impossibilities – all lend the persons and their acts some element of mystery and some suggestion of infinite purposes working themselves out before us. Something similar is apparent in *Macbeth*, a down-pressing, enveloping presence, mysterious and fearful: there it is purely evil, and its nature is personified in the Weird Sisters. Here it has no personal symbol, it is not evil, nor good; neither beautiful, nor ugly. It is purely a brooding presence, vague, inscrutable, enigmatic; a misty blurring opacity stilly overhanging, interpenetrating plot and action. This mysterious accompaniment to the *Lear* story makes of its persons vague symbols of universal forces. But those persons, in relation to their setting, are not vague. They have outline, though few have colour: they are like near figures in a mist. They blend with the quality of the whole. The form of the individual is modified, in tone, by this blurring fog. The *Lear* mist drifts across them as each in turn voices its typical phraseology; for this impregnating reality is composed of a multiplicity of imaginative correspondencies in phrase, thought, action throughout the play. That mental atmosphere is as important, more important sometimes, than the persons themselves; nor, till we have clear sight of this peculiar *Lear* atmosphere, shall we appreciate the fecundity of human creation moving within it. *King Lear* is a work of philosophic vision. We watch, not ancient Britons, but humanity; not England, but the world. Mankind's relation to the universe is its theme, and Edgar's trumpet is as the universal judgement summoning vicious men to account.

MACBETH (1605–1606)

Long regarded as a profound vision of evil, *Macbeth* differs from the other Shakespearean tragedies in that the evil is transferred from the villain to the hero; not that Shakespeare's tragic figures are ever conceived in the simplistic tones of black and white. Although the Elizabethans took liberties with Aristotle's dictum that tragedy does not deal with the overthrow of a bad character, it would be accepted by them that concentration on the evil deed itself does not constitute tragedy. The overtly political theme is clear, and the play has been called the greatest of the moralities. It is Shakespeare's ability to identify, or to portray with an understanding which engages our sympathy, a villainous hero who is not merely a villain which perhaps constitutes the major critical question.

Samuel Johnson
The Plays of Shakespeare (1765)

Johnson's forthright assertion about the detestation of Lady Macbeth *and the rejoicing at the fall of Macbeth would be contested by later writers, who see the redemptive element in the character of Macbeth as the core of the tragedy.*

This play is deservedly celebrated for the propriety of its fictions, and solemnity, grandeur, and variety of its action; but it has no nice discrimination of character, the events are too great to admit the influence of particular dispositions, and the course of the action necessarily determines the conduct of the agents.

The danger of ambition is well described; and I know not whether it may not be said in defence of some parts which now seem improbable, that, in Shakespeare's time, it was necessary to warn credulity against vain and illusive predictions.

The passions are directed to their true end. Lady Macbeth is merely detested; and though the courage of Macbeth preserves some esteem, yet every reader rejoices at his fall.

Charles Lamb
On the Tragedies of Shakespeare (1811)

For Lamb the essence of the tragedy in Macbeth *lies in the poetically suggested atmosphere of horror and evil impulse, readily seized upon*

*by the imagination of the perceptive reader, whereas stage represen-
tation concentrates the mind on the action. Setting aside the anti-
theatrical stance, Lamb's view looks forward to modern critical
approaches which examine Shakespeare's ability to manipulate our
sympathetic response to an apparently negative picture of evil.*

The state of sublime emotion into which we are elevated by those
images of night and horror which Macbeth is made to utter, that
solemn prelude with which he entertains the time till the bell shall
strike which is to call him to murder Duncan, – when we no longer
read it in a book, when we have given up that vantage-ground of
abstraction which reading possesses over seeing, and come to see a
man in his bodily shape before our eyes actually preparing to commit
a murder, if the acting be true and impressive as I have witnessed it in
Mr. K's performance of that part, the painful anxiety about the act,
the natural longing to prevent it while it yet seems unperpetrated, the
too close pressing semblance of reality, give a pain and an uneasiness
which totally destroy all the delight which the words in the book
convey, where the deed doing never presses upon us with the painful
sense of presence: it rather seems to belong to history, – to something
past and inevitable, if it has any thing to do with time at all. The
sublime images, the poetry alone, is that which is present to our
minds in the reading.

William Hazlitt
'Characters of Shakespeare's Plays' (1817)

*The critical theme developed by Hazlitt of the stark contrasts in
Macbeth was to become well established in approaches to the tragedy.
His view of the play's desperate action and reaction, its antitheses of
life and death, good and evil, is a common critical starting-point. In a
typical nineteenth-century approach through character Hazlitt compares Macbeth with Richard III and recognizes the tragic importance
of the inner and outer struggle of Macbeth. There is perhaps a literary
echo from the world of the novel in his comment on what may at first
appear as the 'Gothic outline' of the character of Macbeth, which could
so easily have descended to the melodramatic. In his analysis Hazlitt*

concludes that Shakespeare holds our sympathy appropriately for even this disturbing tragic figure.

Macbeth (generally speaking) is done upon a stronger and more systematic principle of contrast than any other of Shakespeare's plays. It moves upon the verge of an abyss, and is a constant struggle between life and death. The action is desperate and the reaction is dreadful. It is a huddling together of fierce extremes, a war of opposite natures which of them shall destroy the other. There is nothing but what has a violent end or violent beginnings. The lights and shades are laid on with a determined hand; the transitions from triumph to despair, from the height of terror to the repose of death, are sudden and startling; every passion brings in its fellow-contrary, and the thoughts pitch and jostle against each other as in the dark. The whole play is an unruly chaos of strange and forbidden things, where the ground rocks under our feet. Shakespeare's genius here took its full swing, and trod upon the farthest bounds of nature and passion. This circumstance will account for the abruptness and violent antitheses of the style, the throes and labour which run through the expression, and from defects will turn them into beauties. 'So fair and foul a day I have not seen,' &c. 'Such welcome and unwelcome news together.' 'Men's lives are like the flowers in their caps, dying or ere they sicken.' 'Look like the innocent flower, but the serpent under it.' . . .

The leading features in the character of Macbeth are striking enough, and they form what may be thought at first only a bold, rude, Gothic outline. By comparing it with other characters of the same author we shall perceive the absolute truth and identity which is observed in the midst of the giddy whirl and rapid career of events. Macbeth in Shakespeare no more loses his identity of character in the fluctuations of fortune or the storm of passion, than Macbeth in himself would have lost the identity of his person. Thus he is as distinct a being from Richard III as it is possible to imagine, though these two characters in common hands, and indeed in the hands of any other poet, would have been a repetition of the same general idea, more or less exaggerated. For both are tyrants, usurpers, murderers, both aspiring and ambitious, both courageous, cruel, treacherous. But Richard is cruel from nature and constitution. Macbeth becomes so from accidental circumstances. Richard is from his birth deformed in body and mind, and naturally incapable of good. Macbeth is full of 'the milk of human kindness,' is frank, sociable, generous. He is tempted

to the commission of guilt by golden opportunities, by the insti-
gations of his wife, and by prophetic warnings. Fate and metaphysical
aid conspire against his virtue and his loyalty. Richard on the contrary
needs no prompter, but wades through a series of crimes to the height
of his ambition from the ungovernable violence of his temper and a
reckless love of mischief. He is never gay but in the prospect or in the
success of his villainies: Macbeth is full of horror at the thoughts of
the murder of Duncan, which he is with difficulty prevailed on to
commit, and of remorse after its perpetration. Richard has no mixture
of common humanity in his composition, no regard to kindred or to
posterity, he owns no fellowship with others, he is 'himself alone.'
Macbeth is not destitute of feelings of sympathy, is accessible to pity,
is even made in some measure the dupe of his uxoriousness, ranks the
loss of friends, of the cordial love of his followers, and of his good
name, among the causes which have made him weary of life, and
regrets that he has ever seized the crown by unjust means, since he
cannot transmit it to his posterity –

> For Banquo's issues have I fil'd my mind –
> For them the gracious Duncan have I murther'd
> To make them Kings, the seed of Banquo's kings.

In the agitation of his mind, he envies those whom he has sent to
peace. 'Duncan is in his grave; after life's fitful fever he sleeps well.' It
is true, he becomes more callous as he plunges deeper in guilt,
'direness is thus rendered familiar to his slaughterous thoughts' – and
he in the end anticipates his wife in the boldness and bloodiness of his
enterprises, while she for want of the same stimulus of action, 'is
troubled with thick-coming fancies that rob her of her rest,' goes mad
and dies. Macbeth endeavours to escape from reflection of his crimes
by repelling their consequences, and banishes remorse for the past by
the meditation of future mischief. This is not the principle of
Richard's cruelty, which displays the wanton malice of a fiend as
much as the frailty of human passion. Macbeth is goaded on to acts of
violence and retaliation by necessity; to Richard, blood is a pastime. –
There are other decisive differences inherent in the two characters.
Richard may be regarded as a man of the world, a plotting, hardened
knave, wholly regardless of everything but his own ends, and the
means to secure them. – Not so Macbeth. The superstitions of the age,
the rude state of society, the local scenery and customs, all give a
wildness and imaginary grandeur to his character. From the strangeness of the events that surround him, he is full of amazement and
fear; and stands in doubt between the world of reality and the world of

fancy. He sees sights not shewn to mortal eye, and hears unearthly music. All is tumult and disorder within and without his mind; his purposes recoil upon himself, are broken and disjointed; he is the double thrall of his passions and his evil destiny. Richard is not a character either of imagination or pathos, but of pure self-will. There is no conflict of opposite feelings in his breast. The apparitions which he sees only haunt him in his sleep; nor does he live like Macbeth in a waking dream. Macbeth has considerable energy and manliness of character; but then he is 'subject to all the skyey influences.' He is sure of nothing but the present moment. Richard in the busy turbulence of his projects never loses his self-possession, and makes use of every circumstance that happens as an instrument of his long-reaching designs. In his last extremity we can only regard him as a wild beast taken in the toils: while we never entirely lose our concern for Macbeth; and he calls back all our sympathy by that fine close of thoughtful melancholy,

> My way of life is fallen into the sear
> The yellow leaf . . .

Samuel Taylor Coleridge
Lectures on Shakespeare (1818)

Coleridge's comparison of the openings of Macbeth *and* Hamlet *allows him to highlight the direct appeal to the imagination and the emotions which characterizes* Macbeth. *There are few who would now accept Coleridge's rejection of the 'passage of the Porter' (II, iii), a view which may be compared with De Quincey's essay on the knocking at the gate. The psychological insight displayed by Coleridge in his approach to character in* Macbeth *has perhaps been over-praised, but he attempts to understand the mental attitude of the conquering general. Subsequent criticism has been very much concerned with the question of demonology in relation to* Macbeth, *and Coleridge clearly saw the dramatic significance of the witches in the development of the tragedy.*

Macbeth stands in contrast throughout with *Hamlet*; in the manner of the opening more especially. In the latter, there is a gradual ascent from the simplest forms of conversation to the language of impassioned intellect, – yet the intellect still remaining the seat of passion: in the former, the invocation is at once made to the imagination and the emotions connected therein. Hence the movement throughout is the most rapid of all Shakespeare's plays; and hence also, with the exception of the disgusting passage of the Porter (II, iii), which I dare pledge myself to demonstrate to be an interpolation of the actors, there is not, to the best of my remembrance, a single pun or play on words in the whole drama. I have previously given an answer to the thousand times repeated charge against Shakespeare upon the subject of his punning, and I here merely mention the fact of the absence of any puns in *Macbeth*, as justifying a candid doubt at least, whether even in these figures of speech and fanciful modifications of language, Shakespeare may not have followed rules and principles that merit and would stand the test of philosophic contemplation in *Macbeth*, – the play being wholly and purely tragic. For the same cause, there are no reasonings of equivocal morality, which would have required a more leisurely state and a consequently greater activity of mind; – no sophistry of self-delusion, – except only that previously to the dreadful act, Macbeth mistranslates the recoilings and ominous whispers of conscience into prudential and selfish reasonings, and, after the deed done, the terrors of remorse into fear from external dangers, – like delirious men who run away from the phantoms of their own brains, or, raised by terror to rage, stab the real object that is within their reach: – whilst Lady Macbeth merely endeavours to reconcile his and her own sinkings of heart by anticipations of the worst, and an affected bravado in confronting them. In all the rest, Macbeth's language is the grave utterance of the very heart, conscience-sick, even to the last faintings of moral death. It is the same in all the other characters. The variety arises from rage, caused ever and anon by disruption of anxious thought, and the quick transition of fear into it.

In *Hamlet* and *Macbeth* the scene opens with superstition; but, in each it is not merely different, but opposite. In the first it is connected with the best and holiest feelings; in the second with the shadowy, turbulent, and unsanctified cravings of the individual will. Nor is the purpose the same; in the one the object is to excite, whilst in the other it is to mark a mind already excited. Superstition, of one sort or another, is natural to victorious generals; the instances are too notorious to need mentioning. There is so much of chance in warfare, and such vast events are connected with the acts of a single individual, – the representative, in truth, of the efforts of myriads, and yet to the public and, doubtless, to his own feelings, the aggregate of all, – that the proper temperament for generating or receiving superstitious impressions is naturally produced. Hope, the master element of a commanding genius, meeting with an active and combining intellect, and an imagination of just that degree of vividness which disquiets and impels the soul to try to realize its images, greatly increases the creative power of the mind; and hence the images become a satisfying world of themselves, as is the case in every poet and original philosopher: – but hope fully gratified, and yet, the elementary basis of the passion remaining, becomes fear; and, indeed, the general who must often feel, even though he may hide it from his own consciousness, how large a share chance had in his successes, may very naturally be irresolute in a new scene, where he knows that all will depend on his own act and election.

The weird Sisters are as true a creation of Shakespeare's as his Ariel and Caliban, – fates, furies, and materializing witches being the elements. They are wholly different from any representation of witches in the contemporary writers, and yet presented a sufficient external resemblance to the creatures of vulgar prejudice to act immediately on the audience. Their character consists in the imaginative disconnected from the good; they are the shadowy obscure and fearfully anomalous of physical nature, the lawless of human nature, – elemental avengers without sex or kin:

> Fair is foul and foul is fair;
> Hover thro' the fog and filthy air.

Thomas De Quincey
'On the Knocking at the Gate in Macbeth' (1823)

T. S. Eliot described De Quincey's essay on Macbeth *as perhaps the best-known single piece of criticism of Shakespeare that has been written. It is a remarkable record of an intuitive reaction to a scene in the play being translated into a meaningful insight into the heart of the tragedy. For all its ornate prose De Quincey's personal testimony is probably worth more than a great deal of academic erudition, and he makes the important critical point of there being clear evidence of design behind what may appear to some as casual interpolation.*

From my boyish days I had always felt a great perplexity on one point in *Macbeth*. It was this: the knocking at the gate, which succeeds to the murder of Duncan, produced to my feelings an effect for which I never could account. The effect was, that it reflected back upon the murderer a peculiar awfulness and a depth of solemnity; yet, however obstinately I endeavoured with my understanding to comprehend this, for many years I never could see *why* it should produce such an effect.

. . .

But to return from this digression, my understanding could furnish no reason why the knocking at the gate in *Macbeth* should produce any effect, direct or reflected. In fact, my understanding said positively that it could *not* produce any effect. But I knew better; I felt that it did; and I waited and clung to the problem until further knowledge should enable me to solve it. At length, in 1812, Mr. Williams made his *debut* on the stage of Ratcliffe Highway, and executed those unparalleled murders which have procured for him such a brilliant and undying reputation. . . . Now it will be remembered that in the first of these murders (that of the Marrs), the same incident (of a knocking at the door) soon after the work of extermination was complete, did actually occur, which the genius of Shakespeare has invented; and all good judges, and the most eminent dilettanti, acknowledged the felicity of Shakespeare's suggestion, as soon as it was actually realized. Here, then, was a fresh proof that I was right in relying on my own feelings, in opposition to my understanding; and again I set myself to study the problem; at length I solved it to my satisfaction, and my solution is this. Murder, in ordinary cases, where the sympathy is wholly directed to the case of the murdered person, is an incident of coarse and vulgar horror; and for this reason, that it flings the interest exclusively upon the natural but ignoble instinct by which we cleave to life; an instinct which, as being indispensable to the primal law of self-preservation, is the same in kind (though different in degree) amongst all living creatures: this instinct, therefore, because it annihilates all distinctions, and degrades the greatest of men to the level of 'the poor beetle that we tread on,' exhibits human nature in its most abject and humiliating attitude. Such an attitude would little suit the purposes of the poet. What then must he do? He must throw the interest on the murderer. Our sympathy must be with *him* (of course I mean sympathy of comprehension, a sympathy by which we enter into his feelings, and are made to understand them, – not a sympathy of pity or approbation). In the murdered person, all strife of thought, all flux and reflux of passion and of purpose, are crushed by one over-whelming panic; the fear of instant death smites him 'with its petrific mace.' But in the murderer, such a murderer as a poet will condescend to, there must be raging some great storm of passion – jealousy, ambition, vengeance, hatred – which will create a hell within him; and into this hell we are to look.

In *Macbeth*, for the sake of gratifying his own enormous and teeming faculty of creation, Shakespeare has introduced two murderers: and, as usual in his hands, they are remarkably discriminated: but, though in Macbeth the strife of mind is greater than in his wife, the tiger spirit not so awake, and his feelings caught chiefly by contagion from her, – yet, as both were finally involved in the guilt of murder, the murderous mind of necessity is finally to be presumed in both. This was to be expressed; and on its own account, as well as to make it a more proportionable antagonist to the unoffending nature of their victim, 'the gracious Duncan,' and adequately to expound 'the deep damnation of his taking off,' this was to be expressed with peculiar energy. We were to be made to feel that the human nature, i.e. the divine nature of love and mercy, spread through the hearts of all creatures, and seldom utterly withdrawn from man – was gone, vanished, extinct, and that the fiendish nature had taken its place. And, as this effect is marvellously accomplished in the *dialogues* and *soliloquies* themselves, so it is finally consummated by the expedient under consideration; and it is to this that I now solicit the reader's attention. If the reader has ever witnessed a wife, daughter, or sister in a fainting fit, he may chance to have observed that the most affecting moment in such a spectacle is *that* in which a sigh and a stirring announce the recommencement of suspended life. Or, if the reader has ever been present in a vast metropolis, on the day when some great national idol was carried in funeral pomp to his grave, and chancing to walk near the course through which it passed, has felt powerfully in the silence and desertion of the streets, and in the stagnation of ordinary business, the deep interest which at the moment was possessing the heart of man – if all at once he should hear the death-like stillness broken up by the sound of wheels rattling away from the scene, and making known that the transitory vision was dissolved, he will be aware that at no moment was his sense of the complete suspension and pause in ordinary human concerns so full and affecting, as at that moment when the suspension ceases, and the goings-on of human life are suddenly resumed. All action in any direction is best expounded, measured, and made apprehensible, by reaction. Now apply this to the case in *Macbeth*. Here, as I have said, the retiring of the human heart, and the entrance of the fiendish heart was to be expressed and made sensible. Another world has stept in; and the murderers are taken out of the region of human things, human purposes, human desires. They are transfigured: Lady Macbeth is 'unsexed'; Macbeth has forgot that he was born of woman; both are conformed to the image of devils; and the world of devils is suddenly revealed. But how shall this be conveyed and made palpable? In order that a new world may step in, this world must for a time disappear. The murderers, and the murder must be insulated – cut off by an immeasurable gulf from the ordinary tide and succession of human affairs – locked up and sequestered in some deep recess; we must be made sensible that the world of ordinary life is suddenly arrested – laid asleep – tranced – racked into a dread armistice; time must be annihilated; relation to things without abolished; and all must pass self-withdrawn into a deep syncope and suspension of earthly passion. Hence it is, that when the deed is done, when the work of darkness is perfect, then the world of darkness passes away like a pageantry in the clouds: the knocking at the gate is heard; and it makes known audibly that the reaction has commenced; the human has made its reflux upon the fiendish; the pulses of life are beginning to beat again; and the re-establishment of the goings-on of the world in which we live, first makes us profoundly sensible of the awful parenthesis that had suspended them.

O mighty poet! Thy works are not as those of other men, simply and merely great works of art; but are also like the phenomena of nature, like the sun and the sea, the stars and the flowers; like frost and snow, rain and dew, hail-storm and thunder, which are to be studied with entire submission of our own faculties, and in the perfect faith that in them can be no too much or too little, nothing useless or inert – but that, the farther we press in our discoveries, the more we shall see proofs of design and self-supporting arrangement where the careless eye had seen nothing but accident!

A. C. Bradley
Shakespearean Tragedy (1904)

In his approach to Macbeth *Bradley emphasizes not only character, but the atmosphere of darkness, the imagery of colour, and the use of irony in creating a tragedy of stark contrasts. He follows earlier critics in recognizing the dramatic importance of the supernatural elements. In his character-analysis of Macbeth he echoes Hazlitt in seeing evidence of poetic imagination, which helps to provide some sympathy for a villainous tragic hero. This raises a critical point pursued by later critics, who argue that the poetic language developed by the author for the play generally cannot properly be used as evidence in the establishment of individual character. The question becomes involved with the validity of the approach to dramatic character through psychological realism.*

Darkness, we may say even blackness, broods over this tragedy. It is remarkable that almost all the scenes which at once recur to memory take place either at night or in some dark spot. The vision of the dagger, the murder of Duncan, the murder of Banquo, the sleep-walking of Lady Macbeth, all come in night-scenes. The Witches dance in the thick air of a storm, or, 'black and midnight hags,' receive Macbeth in a cavern. The blackness of night is to the hero a thing of fear, even of horror; and that which he feels becomes the spirit of the play. The faint glimmerings of the western sky at twilight are here menacing: it is the hour when the traveller hastes to reach safety in his inn, and when Banquo rides homewards to meet his assassins; the hour when 'light thickens,' when 'night's black agents to their prey do rouse,' when the wolf begins to howl, and the owl to scream, and withered murder steals forth to his work. Macbeth bids the stars hide their fires that his 'black' desires may be concealed; Lady Macbeth calls on thick night to come, palled in the dunnest smoke of hell. The moon is down and no stars shine when Banquo, dreading the dreams of the coming night, goes unwillingly to bed, and leaves Macbeth to wait for the summons of the little bell. When the next day should dawn, its light is 'strangled,' and 'darkness does the face of earth entomb.' In the whole drama the sun seems to shine only twice; first, in the beautiful but ironic passage where Duncan sees the swallows flitting round the castle of death; and, afterwards, when at the close the avenging army gathers to rid the earth of its shame. Of the many slighter touches which deepen this effect I notice only one. The failure of nature in Lady Macbeth is marked by her fear of darkness; 'she has light by her continually.' And in the one phrase of fear that escapes her lips even in sleep, it is of the darkness of the place of torment that she speaks.

The atmosphere of *Macbeth*, however, is not that of unrelieved blackness. On the contrary, as compared with *King Lear* and its cold dim gloom, *Macbeth* leaves a decided impression of colour; it is really the impression of a black night broken by flashes of light and colour, sometimes vivid and even glaring. They are the lights and colours of the thunder-storm in the first scene; of the dagger hanging before Macbeth's eyes and glittering alone in the midnight air; of the torch borne by the servant when he and his lord come upon Banquo crossing the castle-court to his room; of the torch, again, which Fleance carried to light his father to death, and which was dashed out by one of the murderers; of the torches that flared in the hall on the face of the Ghost and the blanched cheeks of Macbeth; of the flames beneath the boiling caldron from which the apparitions in the cavern rose; of the taper which showed to the Doctor and Gentlewoman the wasted face and blank eyes of Lady Macbeth. And, above all, the colour is the colour of blood. It cannot be an accident that the image of blood is forced upon us continually, not merely by the events themselves, but by full descriptions, and even by reiterations of the word in unlikely parts of the dialogue. The Witches, after their first wild appearance, have hardly quitted the stage when there staggers onto it a 'bloody man,' gashed with wounds. His tale is of a hero whose 'brandished steel smoked with bloody execution,' 'carved out a passage' to his enemy, and 'unseam'd him from the nave to the chaps.' And then he tells of a second battle so bloody that the combatants seemed as if they 'meant to bathe in reeking wounds.' What metaphors! . . .

Let us observe another point. The vividness, magnitude, and violence of the imagery in some of these passages are characteristic of *Macbeth* almost throughout; and their influence contributes to form its atmosphere. Images like those of the babe torn smiling from the breast and dashed to death; of pouring the sweet milk of concord into hell; of the earth shaking in fever; of the frame of things disjointed; of sorrows striking heaven on the face, so that it resounds and yells out like syllables of dolour; of the mind lying in restless ecstasy on a rack; of the mind full of scorpions; of the tale told by an idiot, full of sound and fury; – all keep the imagination moving on a 'wild and violent sea,' while it is scarcely for a moment permitted to dwell on thoughts of peace and beauty. In its language, as in its action, the drama is full of tumult and storm. Whenever the Witches are present we see and hear a thunder-storm: when they are absent we hear of ship-wrecking storms and direful thunders; of tempests that blow down trees and churches, castle, palaces and pyramids; of the frightful hurricane of the night when Duncan was murdered; of the blast on which pity rides like a new-born babe, or on which Heaven's cherubim are horsed. There is thus something magnificently appropriate in the cry 'Blow, wind! Come, wrack!' with which Macbeth, turning from the sight of the moving wood of Birnam, bursts from his castle. He was borne to his throne on a whirlwind, and the fate he goes to meet comes on the wings of storm.

Now all these agencies – darkness, the lights and colours that illuminate it, the storm that rushes through it, the violent and gigantic images – conspire with the appearances of the Witches and the Ghost to awaken horror, and in some degree also a supernatural dread. And to this effect other influences contribute. The pictures called up by the mere words of the Witches stir the same feelings, – those, for example, of the spell-bound sailor driven tempest-tost for nine times nine weary weeks, and never visited by sleep night or day; of the drop of poisonous foam that forms on the moon, and, falling to earth, is collected for pernicious ends; of the sweltering venom of the toad, the finger of the babe killed at its birth by its own mother, the tricklings from the murderer's gibbet. In Nature, again, something is felt to be at work, sympathetic with human guilt and supernatural malice. She labours with portents.

> Lamentings heard in the air, strange screams of death,
> And prophesying with accents terrible,

burst from her. The owl clamours all through the night; Duncan's horses devour each other in frenzy; the dawn comes, but no light with it. Common sights and sounds, the crying of crickets, the croak of the raven, the light thickening after sunset, the home-coming of the rooks, are all ominous. Then, as if to deepen these impressions, Shakespeare has concentrated attention on the obscurer regions of man's being, on phenomena which make it seem that he is in the power of secret forces lurking below, and independent of his con-sciousness and will: such as the relapse of Macbeth from conversation into a reverie, during which he gazes fascinated at the image of murder drawing closer; the writing on his face of strange things he never meant to show; the pressure of imagination heightening into illusion, like the vision of a dagger in the air, at first bright, then suddenly splashed with blood, or the sound of a voice that cried 'Sleep no more' and would not be silenced. To these are added other, and constant, allusions to sleep, man's strange, half-conscious life; to the misery of its withholding; to the terrible dreams of remorse; to the cursed thoughts from which Banquo is free by day, but which tempt him in his sleep: and again to abnormal disturbances of sleep; in the two men, of whom one during the murder of Duncan laughed in his sleep, and the other raised a cry of murder; and in Lady Macbeth, who rises to re-enact in somnambulism those scenes the memory of which is pushing her on to madness or suicide. All this has one effect, to excite supernatural alarm and, even more, a dread of the presence of evil not only in its recognised seat but all through and around our mysterious nature. Perhaps there is no other work equal to *Macbeth* in the production of this effect. . . .

Macbeth, the cousin of a King mild, just, and beloved, but now too old to lead his army, is introduced to us as a general of extraordinary prowess, who has covered himself with glory in putting down rebellion and repelling the invasion of a foreign army. In these conflicts he showed great personal courage, a quality which he continues to display throughout the drama in regard to all plain dangers. It is difficult to be sure of his customary demeanour, for in the play we see him either in what appears to be an exceptional relation to his wife, or else in the throes of remorse and desperation; but from his behaviour during his journey home after the war, from his *later* conversations with Lady Macbeth, and from his language to the murderers of Banquo and to others, we imagine him as a great warrior, somewhat masterful, rough, and abrupt, a man to inspire some fear and much admiration. He was thought 'honest,' or honourable; he was trusted, apparently, by everyone; Macduff, a man of the highest integrity, 'loved him well.' And there was, in fact, much good in him. We have no warrant, I think, for describing him, with many writers, as of a 'noble' nature, like Hamlet or Othello; but he had a keen sense both of honour and of the worth of a good name. The phrase, again, 'too full of the milk of human kindness,' is applied to him in impatience by his wife, who did not fully understand him; but certainly he was far from devoid of humanity and pity.

At the same time he was exceedingly ambitious. He must have been so by temper. The tendency must have been greatly strengthened by his marriage. When we see him, it has been further stimulated by his remarkable success and by the consciousness of exceptional powers and merit. It becomes a passion. The course of action suggested by it is extremely perilous: it sets his good name, his position, and even his life on the hazard. It is also abhorrent to his better feelings. Their defeat in the struggle with ambition leaves him utterly wretched, and would have kept him so, however complete had been his outward success and security. On the other hand, his passion for power and his instinct of self-assertion are so vehement that no inward misery could persuade him to relinquish the fruits of crime, or to advance from remorse to repentance.

In the character so far sketched there is nothing very peculiar, though the strength of the forces contending in it is unusual. But there is in Macbeth one marked peculiarity, the true apprehension of which is the key to Shakespeare's conception. This bold ambitious man of action has, within certain limits, the imagination of a poet, – and imagination on the one hand extremely sensitive to impressions of a certain kind, and, on the other, productive of violent disturbance both of mind and body. Through it he is kept in contact with supernatural impressions and is liable to supernatural fears. And through it, especially, come to him the intimations of conscience and honour. Macbeth's better nature – to put the matter for clearness' sake too broadly – instead of speaking to him in the overt language of moral ideas, commands, and prohibitions, incorporates itself in images which alarm and horrify. His imagination is thus the best of him, something usually deeper and higher than his conscious thoughts; and if he had obeyed it he would have been safe. But his wife quite misunderstands it, and he himself understands it only in part. The terrifying images which deter him from crime and follow its commission, and which are really the protest of his deepest self, seem to his wife the creations of mere nervous fear, and are sometimes referred by himself to the dread of vengeance or the restlessness of insecurity. His conscious or reflective mind, that is, moves chiefly among considerations of outward success and failure, while his inner being is convulsed by conscience. And his inability to understand himself is repeated and exaggerated in the interpretations of actors and critics, who represent him as a coward, cold-blooded, calculating, and pitiless, who shrinks from crime simply because it is dangerous, and suffers afterwards simply because he is not safe. In reality his courage is frightful. He strides from crime to crime, though his soul never ceases to bar his advance with shapes of terror, or to clamour in his ears that he is murdering his peace and casting away his 'eternal jewel.'

G. Wilson Knight
The Wheel of Fire (1930)

The psychological reality of character, the handling of plot or the supposed intentions of the author are rejected by Wilson Knight in his approach to Macbeth. *He emphasizes the importance of the poetry in the tragedy, and seeks to illuminate poetic experience in an imaginative interpretation of the play's total impact, rather than critically to probe for apparent inconsistencies and structural weaknesses. This counterpoint to Bradley's character analysis was to have lasting influence on approaches to the play.*

Macbeth is Shakespeare's most profound and mature vision of evil. In the ghost and death themes of *Hamlet* we have something of the same quality; in the Brutus-theme of *Julius Caesar* we have an exactly analogous rhythm of spiritual experience; in *Richard III* we have a parallel history of an individual's crime. In *Macbeth* all this, and the many other isolated units of similar quality throughout Shakespeare, receive a final, perfect, form. Therefore analysis of *Macbeth* is of profound value: but it is not easy. Much of *Hamlet*, and the *Troilus-Othello-Lear* succession culminating in *Timon of Athens*, can be regarded as representations of the 'hate-theme.' We are faced by man's aspiring nature, unsatiated of its desire among the frailties and inconsistencies of its world. They thus point us to good, not evil, and their very gloom of denial is the shadow of a great assertion. They thus lend themselves to interpretation in terms of human thought, and their evil can be regarded as a negation of man's positive longing. In *Macbeth* we find not gloom, but blackness: the evil is not relative, but absolute. In point of imaginative profundity *Macbeth* is comparable alone to *Antony and Cleopatra*. There we have a fiery vision of a paradisal consciousness; here the murk and nightmare torment of a conscious hell. This evil, being absolute and therefore alien to man, is in essence shown as inhuman and supernatural, and is thus most difficult of location in any philosophical scheme. *Macbeth* is fantastical and imaginative beyond other tragedies. Difficulty is increased by that implicit blurring of effects, that palling darkness, that overcasts plot, technique, style. The persons of the play are themselves groping. Yet we are left with an overpowering knowledge of suffocating, conquering evil, and fixed by the basilisk eye of a nameless terror. The nature of this evil will be the subject of my essay.

It is dangerous to abstract the personal history of the protagonist from his environment as a basis for interpretation. The main theme is not primarily differentiated from that of the important subsidiary persons and cannot stand alone. Rather there is a similarity, and the evil of Banquo, Macduff, Malcolm, and the enveloping atmosphere of the play, all form so many steps by which we may approach and understand the titanic evil which grips the two protagonists. The *Macbeth* universe is woven in a texture of a single pattern. The whole play is one swift act of the poet's mind, and as such must be interpreted, since the technique confronts us not with separate integers of 'character' or incident, but with a molten welding of thought with thought, event with event. There is an interpenetrating quality that subdues all to itself. Therefore I shall start by noticing some of the more important elements in this total imaginative effect, and thence I shall pass to the more purely human element. The story and action of the play alone will not carry us far. Here the logic of imaginative correspondence is more significant and more exact than the logic of plot. . . .

The *Macbeth* vision is powerfully superlogical. Yet is is the work of interpretation to give some logical coherence to things imaginative. To do this, it is manifestly not enough to abstract the skeleton of logical sequence which is the story of the play: that is to ignore the very quality which justifies our anxious attention. Rather, relinquishing our horizontal sight of the naked rock-line which is the story, we should, from above, view the whole work extended, spatialized: and then map out imaginative similarities and differences, hills and vales and streams. Only to such a view does *Macbeth* reveal the full riches of its meaning. Interpretation must thus first receive the quality of the play in the imagination, and then proceed to translate this whole experience into a new logic which will not be confined to those superficialities of cause and effect which we think to trace in our own lives and actions, and try to impose on the persons of literature. In this way, we shall know that *Macbeth* shows us an evil not to be accounted for in terms of 'will' and 'causality'; that it expresses its vision, not to a critical intellect, but to the responsive imagination; and, working in terms not of 'character' or any ethical code, but of the abysmal deeps of a spirit-world untuned to human reality, withdraws the veil from the black streams which mill that consciousness of fear symbolized in actions of blood. *Macbeth* is the apocalypse of evil.

4

Later critical texts

In the twentieth century critical approaches to Shakespeare have increased in volume and diversity, and tragedy remains a dominant theme. Critical controversy can be bewildering, and the number of new texts is almost overwhelming. Never before has it been more important to balance first-hand knowledge of the text with judicious exploration of the vast array of critical material available. The standard reference books will provide a ready lead into the critical pursuit. The Modern Language Research Association's *Annual Bibliography of English Language and Literature* will list each year a thousand or so articles and books under William Shakespeare, arranged into editions, general criticism, individual works, and productions of the plays. More useful, perhaps, is the English Association's *Year's Work in English Studies*, which each year summarizes significant critical works under Shakespeare divided into general criticism and sections on each of the plays. There are many annual publications devoted solely to Shakespeare, for example the *Shakespeare Survey* series, which each year takes a specific theme in its approach.

A critical introduction to specific works is most easily obtained from a good modern edition, such as the Arden Shakespeare series, which includes critical survey and considerable textual commentary. All the major tragedies have been edited fairly recently in the series: *Hamlet* by Harold Jenkins in 1982; *Othello* by M. R. Ridley in 1958; *King Lear* by Kenneth Muir in 1972; *Macbeth* by Kenneth Muir in 1962. The earlier tragedies and the Roman tragedies are also available in the series. A more recently developed series is the Oxford Shakespeare, which has the benefit of the latest work in textual scholarship. Apart from the critical introduction, the text carries a full critical apparatus, is modernized according to overall editorial principles, and is characterized by a typographical layout which makes for easy reference.

There are many critical anthologies devoted to Shakespeare generally, as well as to specific works. The Casebook series devotes a volume to each of the plays. All the major tragedies have been included in the series: *Hamlet*, edited by John Jump in 1968; *Othello*, edited by John Wain in 1971; *King Lear*, edited by Frank Kermode in 1969; *Macbeth*, edited by John Wain in 1968. The critical introductions, followed by extracts from early to modern times, provide a useful starting-point for more detailed critical investigation. The most useful collection devoted to a particular theme is *Shakespeare's Tragedies: An Anthology of Modern Criticism*, edited by Laurence Lerner. Modern critical essays on the tragedies from *Romeo and Juliet* to *Timon of Athens* illustrate critical approaches through language and imagery, plot and structural analysis, to the psychology of character. There is a valuable section on the general theme of tragedy, prefaced with the view that the essence of tragedy lies neither in the hero's responsibility nor his redemption but in 'the quality of his defiance' (p. 277). An extract from Friedrich Nietzsche's *Birth of Tragedy* includes the pertinent comment on *Hamlet*: 'Understanding kills action, for in order to act we require the veil of illusion, such is Hamlet's doctrine . . .' (p. 279). T. S. Eliot's famous essay on 'Shakespeare and the Stoicism of Seneca' describes the unity imposed by Shakespeare, an attitude to tragedy derived from Seneca but anticipating Nietzsche. The influence is traced which emerges in Shakespeare as 'a kind of self-consciousness that is new; the self-consciousness and self-dramatization of the Shakespearian hero, of whom Hamlet is only one' (p. 312).

The 'great' tragedies have all been the subject of recent books, but detailed criticism is beyond the scope of the present work. Continued critical interest in the general topic of tragedy is an important element in contemporary approaches to Shakespeare. The decline of tragedy is dramatically stated in George Steiner's influential book *The Death of Tragedy*. This examines the place of tragedy in Western culture and surveys the rise and fall of tragedy from the Greeks through the major languages of Europe to modern times. The difficulty of a precise definition of tragedy is coupled with our undoubted awareness: 'When we say "tragic drama" we know what we are talking about; not exactly, but well enough to recognize the real thing' (p. 9). Apart from placing Shakespearean tragedy within the context of European literature, concepts of tragedy, and alternative genres, there are telling points on Shakespearean criticism. For example, there is a challenge to the modern tendency to read complex political insights into Shakespearean drama where 'the treatment of political action is subordinate to that of the individual dramatic character' (p. 55). Shakespeare's relation to Greek tragedy is examined in the account of the critical influence of G. E. Lessing. Neo-classicism was castigated by Lessing as false criticism, seizing on the dead letter of Greek theory and missing the spirit. Shakespeare belonged with the Greeks: 'the great divide in the history of western drama occurred not between the antique and the Elizabethan, but between Shakespeare and the neo-classics. The *Oresteia* and *Hamlet* belonged together, in the same sphere of tragedy' (p. 189). After the seventeenth century tragedy declined; there was no longer a sense of the supernatural, a superhuman perspective involving divine retribution and predestiny, or of an audience which was part of an organic community. The account of the attitude of the Romantics to tragedy is a valuable complement to their criticism of Shakespeare. The Romantics tended toward self-portrayal, their vehicle the lyric poem, despite their unsuccessful attempts to revivify the drama and their recognition of the power of tragedy. The impersonality of classic art is replaced by the intensification of the personal, and Romanticism is inappropriate to drama. Against this explanation, it is easier to understand the tendency to identify with character, the hero-worship of the author, the attempt to read biographical significance into Shakespeare's heroes. The drama yields to the lyric poem, to be overtaken in its turn after the industrial revolution by the rise of the novel. In great tragedy damnation is real, and divine authority is inescapable, while the Romantic vision is non-tragic and eternally optimistic. In tragedy destiny has to be faced and responsibility accepted, with no materialistic solutions: 'The destiny of Lear cannot be resolved by the establishment of adequate homes for the aged' (p. 128). We live in the age of the happy ending.

Modern criticism of Shakespearean tragedy frequently refers to the elements of Greek tragedy, and to the technical terms which applied to it. There is an explanation of these in Clifford Leech's contribution to the Critical Idiom series: *Tragedy*. The difficulties of precise definition are recognized and modern arguments over a theory of tragedy reviewed. The key terms of 'peripeteia' and 'anagnorisis' are identified – 'peripeteia' is the moment when the action of the tragedy changes its course, a knot or complication having arisen; 'anagnorisis' is the moment of recognition or discovery, the change from ignorance to knowledge, and thus to either love or hate – 'To see things plain – that is *anagnorisis*, and it is the ultimate experience we shall have if we have leisure at the point of death' (p. 65). The basic agreed elements of tragedy suggested are: a change of fortune; a sudden change as likely to have a greater impact; the 'peripeteia' as a special effect of marked ironic force. Nowhere does Shakespeare adhere to the 'unities', but modern writers have surprisingly recognized their value, although not as rules. Tragedy, Leech concludes, is now for a minority audience, who 'stand apart from the drugged world', although 'never, surely, has there been a fuller sense of the tragic end' (p. 80).

The modern perspective of tragedy is also summed up by Geoffrey Brereton in *Principles of Tragedy*, who writes: 'The prestige of tragedy as an intellectual and critical conception stands today in almost inverse ratio to its prestige on the stage' (p. 3). In Brereton's view the approach to character in Shakespeare is to see it as not merely richer than in classical drama but differently motivated. Greek tragedy stresses moral issues which are defined by the actions of the characters, whereas in Shakespeare characters do not so much define the issues as contribute to their creation. Aristotle's category of 'thought' is combined in Shakespearean characters as action and argument; even for the purposes of analysis, 'thought' should not be separated from either 'action' or 'character'. In Shakespeare it is a question not of character-in-action but of character-with-action and 'one must recognize that "thought" is at once an internal action inseparable from the external action and a factor in the composition of "character" ' (p. 95). Shakespeare's tragic characters are thus seen as a new development in the drama, a change from the character as type, and an emphasis on individual power far beyond that recognized by the Greeks. In this modern critical view the psychology of the hero does count, but there is a link with classical theory and practice and some vindication of the earlier critics who saw the importance of character in Shakespeare.

The relationship of Shakespearean to Greek tragedy particularly regarding character is confirmed by Dieter Mehl in *Shakespeare's Tragedies: An Introduction*. This survey of the tragedies explains the variety of character, the sense of individual responsibility, and the absence of 'homiletic soft-soaping'. The question is raised of the validity of modern attempts at a Christian interpretation of the tragedies, or whether George Steiner is correct in seeing both Christianity and Marxism as incompatible with tragedy. This helpful introductory survey comes to the common conclusion that Shakespeare's tragedies are difficult to classify, and exemplifies the resulting critical approach by examining each of the major tragedies in turn.

The English context of Shakespearean tragedy has been increasingly studied in recent years. Early work like Willard Farnham's

Mediaeval Heritage of Elizabethan Tragedy has been carried forward in *The Origins of English Tragedy* by J. M. R. Margeson. Such work has not aimed to identify a distinctive genre of English tragedy, but to examine the nature of the tragic experience as it developed through medieval convention, literary reflection of the classics, and English theatrical practice. Margeson acknowledges the difficulty of explaining why the popular religious and romantic drama as well as the learned drama should move toward tragedy; why several kinds of tragedy emerged at one time, with no dominant form. The common elements in tragedy are classified: the intense exploration of failure and suffering, confrontation with destiny, isolation of a central character, mounting tension of suspense, catastrophe, and emotional resolution. Development through the morality play, chronicle history, and the translations of the 'novelle' or stories from the continent, is traced through the flowering of the Elizabethan playwrights. Retrospectively, it is possible to see the mistake of imposing the abstractions of neo-classical theory on Shakespearean practice. As Margeson observes, the Elizabethans did not occupy themselves with formulating 'ideas of tragedy', either on the basis of practice in the theatre, or of their reading of native, continental, and classical literature. No dominant critical theory influenced the playwrights, and they availed themselves of various modes of interpretation of tragedy, without any inhibiting sense of incongruity. This is the milieu into which Shakespeare was born and developed his art. Historical perspective allows us to see Shakespeare in relation to Kyd, Marlowe, Chapman, and their fellow writers in a remarkable period of dramatic expression; the creative act can be appreciated against its social, religious, philosophical, theatrical, and complex cultural environment. Character delineation in Elizabethan tragedy is seen as a distinctive feature:

> The driving passion that moves Elizabethan tragic characters toward their fatal destiny is one of the most striking qualities of the tragedies. . . . The emotional pattern of Elizabethan tragedy is also vitally dependent upon this element in the drama, the experience of dogged commitment against all odds, a stubborn hanging on to individual will and purpose until some overwhelming climax puts an end to doubt. (p. 185)

The relevance to Shakespearean tragedy needs no further emphasis.

In *English Renaissance Tragedy* T. McAlindon is not primarily concerned with Shakespeare but with the development of sixteenth- and seventeenth-century approaches to tragedy in the work of Kyd,

Marlowe, Tourneur, Webster, and Middleton. Significantly, however, he finds that Shakespeare's tragedies and those of his contemporaries are mutually illuminating. For all the remarkable variety in Elizabethan and Jacobean tragedy, there are discernible common elements and 'Renaissance tragedians found a major stimulus to creative endeavour in each other's work and were quick to borrow and adapt what they saw there' (p. 1). McAlindon denies that the Elizabethan 'World Picture' was the dominating influence that is, the concept of a hierarchical ordering, a 'chain of being' from the lowest orders of life through a stratified humankind to the angels, and a corresponding fear of its disruption. Although brilliantly pictured in Ulysses' famous speech on 'degree' in Shakespeare's *Troilus and Cressida*, this pervasive view was rivalled by another inherited from the Middle Ages and the Greeks. This had polarity as its principle, with the world represented as 'a dialectical structure of strife and amity, discord and concord' (p. 50). For Renaissance dramatists 'tragedy is a form which isolates the moment when that system suddenly shows signs of collapse, with violence, confusion, and wildfire change becoming the dominant facts of experience' (p. 51). It is not argued that the Elizabethans adopted a formula, but rather that they dramatically exploited the opportunities provided by such a world view. They depicted fortune and chance operating in a contrarious world; a providence 'which accommodates the opposites of freedom and necessity and operates through the medium of time to draw justice out of violence and concord out of discord' (p. 51). This uncomfortable cosmology is applied to the work of Shakespeare's contemporaries, but can equally be pursued in Shakespeare's own tragedies and in the 'dark' comedies of *Troilus and Cressida* and *Measure for Measure*. The Senecan influence on Elizabethan tragedy is traced particularly in its attitude to death and suicide, with its overtones of Stoic acceptance. The theme of 'noble death' was developed with dramatic force and rhetoric, and Aristotle's 'recognition' became a component, for at the moment of his fall the hero's understanding reached its peak. This convention modifies the need to search for Christian doctrinal attitudes to self-slaughter, for example in *Hamlet*. The 'sweet violence' of Renaissance tragedy is expressed above all in the theme of revenge, brilliantly exploited from Seneca through Kyd to Shakespeare and others. This Renaissance view of tragedy with its contrarieties affects the apprehension of characterization. Villains are opposite to what they 'seem', advocating unity and sowing discord, and Hamlet's obsession with the word is pregnant with meaning; the tragic heroes oscillate between extremes of feeling and conduct: 'They are thrown into a state of intellectual and moral confusion verging on madness, find it impossible to distinguish between right and wrong, friend and foe; they feel betrayed, but betray themselves' (p. 51). Further critical points emerge from this historical view: against the Elizabethan use of traditional psychology, their microcosmology, attempts to use modern depth psychology are misleading; the skilful use of word-play by Renaissance dramatists is important in establishing the nature of tragic reality. Shakespeare's punning has more dramatic utility than is sometimes recognized.

No modern general theory of tragedy has found acceptance, but many critics have searched for common elements in Shakespeare's tragedies. Bradley's elevation of the four 'great' tragedies to special status has been questioned, but the assessment of Shakespeare's achievement in tragedy has involved the identification of distinctive qualities in the mature tragedies. Bernard McElroy in *Shakespeare's Mature Tragedies*, after close examination of *Hamlet, Othello, King Lear,* and *Macbeth*, finds a common denominator in the collapse of the 'world view' of each of the titular heroes. Fundamental values are undermined, and the subjective world of the hero is devastated. It is argued that this pattern, although adumbrated in *Titus Andronicus*, is not present in the other early tragedies nor in the Roman tragedies, although there are interesting parallels with the political world of *Richard II*. The four tragedies are seen as becoming progressively grimmer. Since the central theme of the tragedies is how the unendurable is to be endured, this is applied in *Hamlet* and *Othello* to particular situations. In the 'most titanic tragedy' of *King Lear*, however, the unendurable is the human condition itself, and medieval Christian assurances have been removed. Hamlet and Othello can come to terms with this world, in situations resolved by their deaths, but 'For Lear, the tragedy is life; death is deliverance from the rack' (p. 242). His world grants neither quarter nor asylum. The world of *Macbeth* is even grimmer because the Christian assurances have been left intact and made the premises of the tragedy. This is not a despairing statement by Shakespeare, but a dramatization of the grim potentialities of the human condition. *Macbeth* is the most 'internalized' of the plays, and Macbeth, who is his own strongest adversary, sees his situation unflinchingly: 'Macbeth is strongly impelled to evil, but he is no less strongly impelled to abhor evil. Hence, he comes to abhor himself' (p. 237). In the evil world of *Macbeth*, 'justice becomes little more than tragic necessity. Its pyrrhic victory is retributive but not redemptive' (p. 215). Macbeth's own death is almost incidental. This gloomy view of the direction of the mature tragedies is contrary to the redemptive interpretation of *Macbeth*. McElroy does not look for a biographical explanation, or a particular historical mood. He admits that the essence of tragedy remains a mystery, but considers that the four tragedies can be taken as an imaginative whole, a single unit of tragic expression. The common element is the heroic struggle to come to terms with a complex reality after basic assumptions have been destroyed. But statements, messages, moral conclusions, or tragic formulae are not implied: 'Shakespeare's emphasis is invariably upon the problem rather than the solution, and the substance of his tragedy is not the outcome of the struggle, but the struggle itself' (p. 243).

In contrast Kenneth Muir in *Shakespeare's Tragic Sequence* rejects Bradley's designation of the four 'great' tragedies as 'pure tragedies' or a distinctive category: 'There is no such thing as Shakespearian Tragedy: there are only Shakespearian tragedies' (p. 12). Nevertheless, Bradley's critical contribution is not to be dismissed out of hand, provided critical examination is concentrated on individual plays without any attempt to apply Aristotelian or other external rules. The critical hammering which Bradley has received has been severe, and Muir cites Lily B. Campbell's *Shakespeare's Tragic Heroes* for its authoritative objection to Bradley's un-historical approach to his subject. In this work Elizabethan psychology is used to demonstrate that Shakespeare's tragic heroes were slaves of passion: Lear of wrath in old age, Macbeth of fear. But, as Muir comments, even if Shakespeare can be shown to be circumscribed by the theories of his age, the resulting view is narrow; it is certainly not in accordance with generations of critical discernment. Attempts to group the tragedies are cited. Harold S. Wilson in *On the Design of Shakespearian Tragedy* postulated three classifications: exemplifying the order of faith are *Romeo and Juliet* and *Hamlet* as thesis, and *Othello* and *Macbeth* as antithesis; exemplifying the order of nature are *Julius Caesar* and *Coriolanus* as thesis and *Timon of Athens* and *Troilus and Cressida* as antithesis; *Antony and Cleopatra* and *King Lear* provide the synthesis. The chronological oddities of this grouping indicate the strain imposed by attempts to discover a unifying pattern of tragedy. A combination of Aristotelian principles deepened by Christian concepts was the unifying theme put forward by Roy W. Battenhouse in *Shakespearean Tragedy: Its Art and its Christian Premises*. This gives rise to such perceptions as a self-righteous Cordelia, and the Ghost in *Hamlet* as coming from hell. T. R. Henn in *The Harvest of Tragedy* concluded that the theme of Shakespearean tragedy was essentially the emergence of evil through personality into an act. As

Muir objects, this is not a distinctive feature of Shakespearean tragedy; evil exists in the tragedies apart from the tragic hero and there are enormous differences between the tragedies. The Christian interpretation of the tragedies is stressed in Virgil K. Whitaker's *The Mirror up to Nature: The Technique of Shakespeare's Tragedies*. The argument here is that the Aristotelian tragic error becomes a moral error, or act of sin, and 'the tragic poet could so simplify his action as to trace cause and effect with dreadful clarity and thereby to provide a powerful moral *exemplum*' (p. 16). Muir accepts that Shakespeare used Christian ideas but notes this did not differentiate him from his fellow tragedians, and pointedly wonders 'if Shakespeare, like some of his critics, regarded the love of Romeo and Juliet as sinful' (p. 16). The critical reaction against attempts to find a unifying principle in Shakespearean tragedy and the over-emphasis on Christian and didactic patterns is voiced by Muir. He also rejects division of the plays into phased periods with biographical significance, concluding that Shakespeare wrote a series of tragedies 'because tragedy was regarded as the highest form of drama and because he felt at the height of his powers' (p. 18). Perhaps the modification to suggest is that Shakespeare seized all opportunities to write plays; he probably never saw himself as a great tragedian.

The rejection of any meaningful grouping of Shakespeare's tragedies or unifying theory is also a feature of E. A. J. Honigmann's approach in *Shakespeare: Seven Tragedies* subtitled *The Dramatic Manipulation of Response*, and he takes the tragedies from *Julius Caesar* in chronological order, referring to the four 'great' tragedies as 'the central tragedies'. The approach is a return to the analysis of dramatic character, but perceived in the multi-faceted way presented by Shakespeare, exploring the modern concern with audience response and the extent to which it was manipulated. This is a considerable advance on the 'realistic' school of theatrical artifice. Bradley's stress on the importance of character is modified:

> Whilst no self-respecting critic will henceforth wish to place Shakespeare's stage-persons on a psychiatrist's couch, to fish in imagined minds for a poet that never was, a psychological or "natural" bias still remains appropriate when we discuss a play's life-like characters. (p. 4)

The critical trend is away from a fixed view of character, toward a recognition of changing perspectives and dramatic techniques. Shakespeare's audience was encouraged to respond creatively, and their perception of the tragic hero was 'a swirl of conflicting impressions' which Shakespeare 'conjured forth and controlled with the utmost care'. Through devices like the soliloquy we think we 'glimpse the ghost in the machine' (p. 11), yet paradoxically, Shakespeare also goes to great lengths to make his tragic hero inaccessible. Despite modern reaction against Hamlet's 'unhealthy sensibility' – T. S. Eliot's complaint about emotion in excess of the facts – we can still become involved in his uncertainties, can trust his sensibility, and can respond with sympathy to his tragic predicament. Despite F. R. Leavis's development of a view, hinted at by Schlegel and bolstered by sociology, that Othello is too easily jealous, we can still respond to one who is both noble Moor and brutal egoist; in Lear we can see royalty coexistent with a foolish old man. The more Shakespeare stretched the tragic hero, the more powerful the tragic effect. There is no theory of tragedy here, but a pointed reference to seven plays called tragedies, separately approached but with common techniques revealed as creating the dramatic effect. Aristotle's catharsis, emphasizing pity and terror, is not found appropriate for Shakespeare, but each of the plays is observed to have an emotional effect at the close. Although audience response channelled through character is the critical mode adopted, this is explained as a matter of critical convenience, not an argument that character should always come first in the investigation of Shakespeare's tragedies.

Modern techniques of criticism have been particularly concerned with the language of the text, seen as a multiple code which needs to be deciphered, its signifying keys uncovered. Critical analysis identifies the author with his text, transforms the author into a linguistic code to be interpreted in ways which deliberately avoid conventionally established modes. John Bayley points out in his introduction to *Shakespeare and Tragedy* that this linguistically related criticism has been applied to continental writers and to novelists like Henry James rather than to Shakespeare, but that Shakespearean critical practice in fact has long employed such methods. Critics of Shakespeare have looked for his code of significance, and 'understood and interpreted him according to their own lights and their own ideas of enjoyment' (p. 1). Bayley argues that the modern critical concept of 'code' corresponds somewhat to Maurice Morgann's term 'impression', so that when Morgann in his famous essay on Falstaff saw him as man of courage rather than buffoon he had in modern critical parlance 'cracked the code' of Shakespeare's text. The impression we receive from Shakespeare's tragedies is that the tragic form exists as a means of giving its freedom to every other aspect of life and art. Shakespearean tragedy acts as a catalyst, its code leading outward to other worlds. The tragedies are not a uniform body, do not exemplify the genre, and lack the formality of action of Greek tragedy. In Shakespeare the imminence of action brings the consciousness of the protagonist into prominence: 'The tragedy itself may be bounded in a nutshell, but the minds of Hamlet, of Macbeth and Othello, make them kings of infinite space.' This 'usurpation of the mind of both practical action and purposeful idea in tragedy' (p. 6) is taken as the most important feature of Shakespeare's relation to tragic form. The critical approach through the transcendence of the consciousness of dramatic character requires a detailed analysis of the individual plays, with *King Lear* seen as 'off key' and *Hamlet*, *Othello* and *Macbeth* grouped as 'Tragedy of Consciousness'. Exploration of the impressions available to the imaginative perception through Shakespeare's 'secret freedom' is a modern replacement of Bradley, with freedom of interpretation linked to Shakespeare's relationship with tragic form and the distinctive nature of Shakespeare's achievement in tragedy.

A more radical view of Shakespearean tragedy than that which appears to return to a modification of Bradley's emphasis on character has been adopted by critics influenced by continental theories. In particular it has been objected that Shakespearean criticism has been influenced by cultural restraints which have interpreted his works merely as a reflection of a prevailing ethos. The philosophical arguments behind new theories are complex, but generally the liberal humanist view of Shakespeare is rejected, while the revolutionary materialism of a Bertold Brecht is favoured. Thus in *Radical Tragedy* Jonathan Dollimore shows how greatly Shakespeare influenced Brecht, who saw correspondences between Elizabethan drama and his own alternative or 'epic' theatre. Brecht objected to the traditional form of theatre, which disguised the fact that it was fabricated or ideologically structured, and enthralled the audience rather than encouraged it to become critically aware. The 'epic' theatre deliberately incorporates contradictions: rather than capturing an audience in one enveloping view it encourages multiple versions of events. Traditional dramatic elements are modified: 'Actors *show* rather than *become* the characters they play; different genres are juxtaposed, sometimes jarringly so' (p. 64). What Brecht calls 'estrangement', sometimes called 'alienation', draws attention to the play as theatre, causes the spectator not to see characters as unalterable, delivered to their fate. People are seen as conditioned by their history, and estrangement uses dialectical materialism which 'treats social situations as processes, and traces out all their inconsistencies' (p. 64). No pre-ordained view of reality is accepted, and nothing exists except in so far as it changes or 'is in disharmony with itself' (p. 64). Epic theatre does not reproduce the conditions of a world view as conceived by traditional criticism, but rather exposes them to critical analysis. Without pursuing the validity of this critique, it is clear that the trend of such criticism is a conscious resistance to established attitudes, particularly those which relate literature to a national-cultural ideal. Tragedy with its established prestige, and Shakespearean tragedy in particular, is obviously a central issue. In the introduction to *Alternative Shakespeares* John Drakakis writes: 'The "alternative" Shakespeares which emerge resist, by virtue of a collective commitment to the principle of contestation of meaning, assimilation into any of the dominant traditions of Shakespeare criticism' (p. 24). In the approach to tragedy, as to other aspects of Shakespeare, the laxity of traditional pluralist approaches with their multiplicity of subjective readings are rejected as 'wholly inadequate as responses to the challenges now proposed by theoretically informed modes of criticism' (p. 25). In the same volume Christopher Norris writes on 'Post-structuralist Shakespeare: Text and Ideology' and takes approaches to tragedy as examples of the tendentious nature of traditional criticism. He describes the way Shakespeare studies are 'inscribed with the national culture' and examines the way that critics have 'looked to Shakespeare for linguistic intimations of an "Englishness" identified as true native vigour and unforced, spontaneous creativity' (p. 49). He finds in Johnson's famous Preface to *The Plays of William Shakespeare* inconsistencies and contradictions which he deduces are caused by the constraints and prejudices of the dominant ideology to which Johnson subscribed. The shifting viewpoint of such criticism is caused by the need to rewrite Shakespeare 'on their own preferred terms of imaginative "truth" ' (p. 56). Johnson is identified as one of the initiators of the long-held notion that literature, identified with culture, is the paradigm of healthy creativity; it follows that Shakespeare holds a special place, and that the tragedies represent the supreme expression of all that is best in a national culture. F. R. Leavis was famous some decades ago for his polemical support of a culture based upon literature (as he conceived it); Norris examines his well-known criticism of *Othello* because it not only seeks to interpret the play, but sets out to be a test case for the responsive reading of a complex text, exemplifying the cultural heroics toward which aspiring readers were directed. Bradley's view of Iago as the arch-villain and Othello as the nobly suffering counterpart is scorned by Leavis, who dismisses it as sentimental. What Norris seeks to demonstrate is that in coming to such different conclusions these two critics become themselves oddly intertwined with the drama played out between Othello and Iago. The same text supports different interpretations, and Freudian psychology can be used to explain the partial under-standing of a literary text by different critics whose unconscious prejudices produce tell-tale symptoms. Critics espouse one side or another of an argument and suppress or unconsciously distort textual evidence which disagrees with their critical reading. An awareness of this state of affairs is claimed as the feature of the new criticism: 'Post-structuralism is perhaps best characterized by its willingness to acknowledge this predicament, rather than set itself up as a "meta-language" ideally exempt from the puzzles and perplexities of literary texts' (p. 61). The Johnson–Leavis era is summed up as 'an effort of ideological containment, an attempt to harness the unruly energies of the text to a stable order of significance' (p. 66). The Victorian attitude to Shakespeare could be cited, where heroes and heroines become identified with real life, and texts need to be Bowdlerized or cleaned up. The post-structuralist move to free texts from surround-ing external restraints is summed up by Norris:

> Shakespeare's meaning can no more be reduced to the currency of liberal-humanist faith than his text to the wished-for con-dition of pristine, uncorrupt authority. All we have are the readings which inevitably tell such partial and complicated stories of their own devising. (p. 66)

Associated with new critical theories are feminist approaches which examine the way social attitudes to women have changed, and the effect of these changes upon approaches to Shakespearean characters such as Ophelia. Critical approaches to tragedy now include linguistic analysis, what is sometimes termed characterology, theories of rhetoric, new apprehensions of Elizabethan and Jacobean society, reappraisal of historical, political, and theatrical interpretation. There is no lack of radicalism in contemporary approaches, but this is preferable to comfortable uniformity or studied indifference. Thus Terry Eagleton in *William Shakespeare* uses Marxism, feminism, and semiotics in his criticism. Shakespeare's language is shown to subvert the very order and stability which the plays seem to uphold, and the problem of reconciling the world to be signified with the word as signifier is revealed in the critical evaluation. Provocatively, *Macbeth* is alleged to have the witches as heroines, and Lady Macbeth is described as the villain of the piece, 'a "bourgeois feminist" who strives to outdo in domination and virility the very male system which subordinates her' (p. 6). The technical complexities of new critical theory, compounded by translation problems with continental originators, can be daunting. However, the spectator is not forgotten in current approaches to Shakespearean tragedy, and the emotional involvement of the audience and the theatrical experience of Shakespeare are also part of the contemporary critical scene. P. A. Jorgensen in *William Shakespeare: The Tragedies* insists that the passion of the tragedies should be felt by the audience, and returns to the Romantic insistence that the genuine response of feeling is superior to merely intellectual reaction. New approaches have not banished the best of past criticism, which claims attention for its moderating perspective. A. C. Bradley's *Shakespearean Tragedy* has been newly issued with an introduction by J. R. Brown, who himself countered the reaction to Bradley, with its emphasis on verse and the supposed doctrines of Shakespeare, with his claim in *Shakespeare's Plays in Performance* 'that Shakespeare's art can never be represented by the printed text of his dialogue, his intention never explained by simple quotation' (p. 162) but must be fully realized in the theatre.

Shakespearean tragedy may be questioned as a distinctive genre, but the tragedies continue to sustain the reinterpretation which is said to be the mark of the classic. Despite intense critical interest, no theory of tragedy emerges as supreme and no definitive version of the plays is likely to gain universal acceptance. Shakespeare has been set against Aristotelian poetics, Romantic enthusiasm, and Brechtian politics but seldom found wanting. The intensity of the critical ferment and the difficulty of encompassing within its purview Shakespeare's achievement is a recognition of the creative power of the tragedies. Shakespeare wrote as a theatrical opportunist, not as a literary theorist. Any theatrical practitioner knows that each production, indeed each living performance, requires new creative responses. These responses include members of the audience, who in re-creation will ensure that Shakespeare lives.

Bibliography

Aristotle, *The Poetics*, tr. Ingram Bywater (Oxford UP; 1909).

Battenhouse, Roy W., *Shakespearean Tragedy: Its Art and its Christian Premises* (Indiana UP; Bloomington, 1969).

Bayley, John, *Shakespeare and Tragedy* (Routledge & Kegan Paul; London, 1981).

Bradbrook, M. C., *Themes and Conventions of Elizabethan Tragedy* (Cambridge UP; 1935).

Bradley, A. C., *Shakespearean Tragedy* (Macmillan; London, 1904); with a new introduction by J. R. Brown (Macmillan; London, 1985).

Brereton, Geoffrey, *Principles of Tragedy* (Routledge & Kegan Paul; London, 1968).

Brooke, Nicholas, *Shakespeare's Early Tragedies* (Methuen; London, 1968).

Brown, J. R., *Shakespeare's Plays in Performance* (Edward Arnold; London, 1966).

Campbell, Lily B., *Shakespeare's Tragic Heroes* (Cambridge UP; 1930).

Charlton, H. B., *Shakespearian Tragedy* (Cambridge UP; 1948).

Clemen, Wolfgang, *The Development of Shakespeare's Imagery* (Methuen; London, 1951).

Coleridge, Samuel Taylor, *Biographia Literaria*, ed. Arthur Symons (Dent; London, 1906).

-- *Lectures on Shakespeare*, ed. Arthur Symons (Dent; London, 1907).

Dollimore, Jonathan, *Radical Tragedy* (Harvester; Brighton, 1984).

Dowden, Edward, *Shakspere: A Critical Study of his Mind and Art* (Routledge & Kegan Paul; London 1875).

Drakakis, John (ed.), *Alternative Shakespeares* (Methuen; London, 1985).

Dryden, John, *Dramatic Poesy and Other Essays* (Dent; London, 1912).

Eagleton, Terry, *William Shakespeare* (Blackwell; Oxford, 1986).

English Association, *Year's Work in English Studies* (John Murray; London, annually).

Evans, Bertrand, *Shakespeare's Tragic Practice* (Oxford UP: 1978).

Farnham, Willard, *The Mediaeval Heritage of Elizabethan Tragedy* (Blackwell; Oxford, 1936).

Frye, Northrop, *Fools of Time: Studies in Shakespearian Tragedy* (Toronto UP; 1967).

Fyfe, W. Hamilton, *Aristotle's Art of Poetry* (Oxford UP; 1940).

Granville-Barker, Harley, *Prefaces to Shakespeare* (Batsford; London, 1958).

Harbage, Alfred, *Shakespeare: The Tragedies* (Prentice-Hall; Englewood Cliffs, 1964).

Hazlitt, William, *Lectures on English Poets* (Dent; London, 1910).

Henn, T. R., *The Harvest of Tragedy* (Methuen; London, 1956).

Holloway, John, *The Story of Night: Studies in Shakespeare's Major Tragedies* (Routledge & Kegan Paul; London, 1961).

Honigmann, E. A. J., *Shakespeare: Seven Tragedies: The Dramatic Manipulation of Response* (Macmillan; London, 1976).

Jenkins, Harold (ed.), *Hamlet*, Arden Shakespeare (Methuen; London, 1982).

Jones, Edmund D. (ed.), *English Critical Essays* (Oxford UP; 1922).

Jones, Ernest, 'The Oedipus Complex as an Explanation of Hamlet's Mystery', in *Hamlet and Oedipus* (Gollancz & Norton; London, 1949).

Jorgensen, P. A., *William Shakespeare: The Tragedies* (Twayne; Boston 1985).

Jump, John (ed.), *Hamlet: A Casebook* (Macmillan; London, 1968).

Kermode, Frank (ed.), *King Lear: A Casebook* (Macmillan; London, 1969).

Knight, G. Wilson, *The Wheel of Fire* (Oxford UP; 1930).

Krook, Dorothea, *Elements of Tragedy* (Yale UP; 1969).

Lawlor, John, *The Tragic Sense in Shakespeare* (Chatto & Windus; London, 1960).

Leech, Clifford, *Shakespeare's Tragedies* (Chatto & Windus; London, 1950).

-- *Tragedy*, Critical Idiom (Methuen; London, 1969).

Lerner, Laurence (ed.), *Shakespeare's Tragedies: An Anthology of Modern Criticism* (Penguin; Harmondsworth, 1963).

McAlindon, T., *English Renaissance Tragedy* (Macmillan; London, 1986).

McElroy, Bernard, *Shakespeare's Mature Tragedies* (Princeton UP; 1973).

Margeson, J. M. R., *The Origins of English Tragedy* (Oxford UP; 1967).

Mehl, Dieter, *Shakespeare's Tragedies: An Introduction* (Cambridge UP; 1986).

Modern Humanities Research Association, *Annual Bibliography of English Language and Literature* (MHRA; London, annually).

Morris, Ivor, *Shakespeare's God: The Role of Religion in the Tragedies* (Allen & Unwin; London, 1972).

Muir, Kenneth (ed.), *King Lear*, Arden Shakespeare (Methuen; London, 1972).

-- *Macbeth*, Arden Shakespeare (Methuen; London, 1962).

-- *Shakespeare Survey 20: Shakespearian and Other Tragedy* (Cambridge UP; 1967).

-- *Shakespeare's Tragic Sequence* (Hutchinson; London, 1972).

Raleigh, Walter, *Shakespeare* (Macmillan; London, 1907).

Ribner, Irving, *Patterns in Shakespearean Tragedy* (Methuen; London, 1960).

Ridler, Anne (ed.), *Shakespeare Criticism 1919-1935* (Oxford UP; 1936).

Ridley, M. R. (ed.), *Othello*, Arden Shakespeare (Methuen; London, 1958).

Sherbo, Arthur (ed.), *Johnson on Shakespeare* (Yale UP; 1965).

Smith D. Nichol (ed.), *Shakespeare Criticism 1623-1840* (Oxford UP; 1916).

Spurgeon, Caroline, *Shakespeare's Imagery and What it Tells Us* (Cambridge UP; 1935).

Steiner, George, *The Death of Tragedy* (Faber; London, 1961).

Stewart, J. I. M., *Character and Motive in Shakespeare* (Longman; Harlow, 1949).

Stoll, Elmer Edgar, *Art and Artifice in Shakespeare* (Cambridge UP; 1933).

Vickers, Brian (ed.), *Shakespeare: The Critical Heritage*, 6 vols (Routledge & Kegan Paul; London, 1981).

Wain, John (ed.), *Macbeth: A Casebook* (Macmillan; London, 1968).

-- *Othello: A Casebook* (Macmillan; London, 1971).

Whitaker, Virgil K., *The Mirror up to Nature: The Technique of Shakespeare's Tragedies* (Huntington Library; Los Angeles 1965).

Wilson, Harold S., *On the Design of Shakespearian Tragedy* (Toronto UP; 1957).

Wilson, J. Dover, *What Happens in Hamlet* (Cambridge UP; 1935).